Praise for *The Tell Me More Gesture*

"Reading *The Tell Me More Gesture* is like having Janet Rowles as your personal guide to improving your relationships. Janet's user-friendly model, as well as her warmth and transparency, both teach and inspire us to welcome conflict. If you have conflict in your life, and who doesn't, reading *The Tell Me More Gesture* is essential."

> —Marshall Goldsmith, world-renowned business educator and coach, and author of the *New York Times* bestsellers, *Triggers, MOJO,* and *What Got You Here Won't Get You There*

"Listening doesn't just resolve conflict, 'It creates us,' said writer Brenda Ueland, 'makes us unfold and expand.' In her brave and wise guide, *The Tell Me More Gesture* author Janet Rowles carries the torch lit by Ueland and shines a light on putting the power of listening to practical use. Conflict? Bring it on!"

> —Eric Utne, founder, *Utne Reader*

"Janet Rowles has devised an ingenious method of using mediation skills for one's own personal use to help not merely resolve conflict, but actually transform it. This is a practical manual for improving personal and professional interactions alike. Janet's book takes a step-by-step approach to finding deeper understanding and resolution with people in our everyday lives. If you want to enrich your relationships, then read and practice *The Tell Me More Gesture!*"

> —M.J. Bauer, Executive Director, Conflict Resolution Center and Board Member of Community Mediation Minnesota.

"We are all smart enough to problem solve situations, but problem solving doesn't resolve conflict. *The Tell Me More Gesture* is a very valuable work for everyone from professionals to couples to families to neighbors to on and on. I can't wait to share it and practice it more."

> —Bill Baker, crisis counselor and educator of marginalized and special needs students, Buena Vista, CO

"Janet Rowles' *The Tell Me More Gesture* encourages us to welcome conflict, and to "listen in such a way that the speaker feels free." Rowles explains the value of helping the people we're in conflict with to thoroughly share their perspective. And she gives us techniques to practice that help us help our adversary get to a better place. This seemingly paradoxical idea, that when in conflict we should *help* the other side, arises from Rowles' understanding of transformative conflict theory. Rowles' insight will also be helpful to professionals in the world of conflict resolution, who too often try to re-direct or contain conflict, when supporting it would lead to much better results. Rowles provides a deep understanding of how conflict works, beyond problem-solving, beyond win/win, to the relational dynamics that determine whether disagreements will turn into war or into meaningful, connecting conversations. While she asks us to take responsibility for how we respond to even the harshest attacks, she acknowledges that it's not so easy and that we need to do our own work to keep ourselves in a strong and compassionate place. Anyone interested in human conflict will find this book inspiring, refreshing, and challenging."

> —Dan Simon practices and teaches transformative mediation in Los Angeles and Saint Paul. He is a board member and fellow of the Institute for the Study of Conflict Transformation and a Certified Transformative Mediator. He writes the blog at both transformativemediation.org and transformativemediation.com.

THANK you so much, Eric.

Janet Rowles

THE
TELL ME MORE
GESTURE

HOW & WHY
TO WELCOME CONFLICT

JANET W. ROWLES, M.A.

OUT-AND-OUT PRESS

Out-and-Out Press
7101 York Ave. So. #157
Minneapolis, MN 55435

Printed in the United States of America

ISBN-13: 978-1-54562-727-3

To my children, Rachel and Adam,
my inspiration to do better everyday,
with gratitude and love.

ACKNOWLEDGMENTS

Thank you to the many and dear individuals who attended workshops, gave feedback, and cheered me on to the completion of this book. In particular, I give great thanks to my brother, Fred Weiner, best developmental editor ever, and to my father, Howard Weiner, for his knowledge of grammar, as well as his interest and loving support. Thank you to Bridget Ryan, who went well beyond duty in finding ways to praise and challenge my thinking and writing; to Pam Arnold, Bill Baker, Adam Collins, Rachel Collins, Jane Friedman, Charlotte Ketchum, Patricia Neal, Linda Reiss, Dan Rowles, and Dan Simon for valuable edits, comments, and encouragement; and to Baruch Bush and Joe Folger for introducing me to the transformative framework of mediation via *The Promise of Mediation* (2005). Cover design by Sinem Erkas. Interior design by Benjamin Seyler. Production by Mill City Press.

CONTENTS

INTRODUCTION

Let's be honest: No one likes conflict. Although it can be exhilarating to watch a suspenseful drama on television or rewarding to console a friend with troubles, we do not look forward to conflict in our own lives. Conflict is messy. Conflict can feel chaotic and scary. Sometimes it is loud, ugly, and exhausting. So why would anyone intentionally welcome conflict? Because difficulties are opportunities to understand each other more deeply. They are the things that give meaning to our lives. Conflict is an essential and unavoidable part of experiencing life to its fullest.

> **Difficulties are opportunities to go deeper. They are the things that give meaning to our lives.**

Welcoming conflict is what I do professionally. I am a mediator, and I accept only high-conflict or emotionally difficult cases. Being comfortable around conflict is an important foundation for a quality mediation practice. When people come into my office, and trust me with difficult and sad and sometimes explosive situations, I do not judge them. Indeed, I welcome the conflict. But here is the catch:

The patient, professional, nonjudgmental, welcoming-conflict me is not the whole me.

A decade ago, I was at a board retreat where we were each asked the question, "What is your vocation or calling?" My response was, "I'm a mediator slash instigator." Everyone laughed, but it is true. I tend to be outspoken and transparent. I am accepting and calm as a mediator, but in the rest of my life I can be opinionated and emotional. This is the instigator side of me.

While it appears ironic that the mediator in professional life creates conflict in personal life, it actually makes perfect sense. Of course everyone has conflicts, even mediators. The interesting part is that the instigator in me, who might make others uncomfortable or cause hurt feelings, also makes me good at the work I do. I have empathy for people who are in conflict, and I do not judge them because I know what conflict feels like firsthand.

> I am not afraid of storms for I am learning how to sail my ship.
>
> —Louisa May Alcott,
> *Little Women*

I began thinking, *I want to feel, in my own conflicts, the same way that I feel around others' conflicts.* So the seeds were sown for an investigation into ways that I can use my mediator skills and apply them to my personal interactions. It was relatively easy for me to welcome conflict at the mediation table, but could I do it in my own life? Could I learn to welcome conflict when I am *in* the conflict?

I considered ways to adapt the concepts I had learned and mediation skills I had developed based on the groundbreaking work of Bush and

Folger (2005) in the transformative approach to mediation. I studied and practiced how to intervene on my own behalf when a neutral third party is not present. I discovered that, indeed, the concepts transfer to personal conflicts. I also learned that understanding the concepts and accomplishing them are very different tasks. So the next work for me was, and is, the practice of recognizing and discarding my well-ingrained reactions in the midst of conflict and replacing them with the mediator skills that have served me well professionally.

> The mind determines what is possible. The heart surpasses it.
>
> —Pilar Coolinta

When I started sharing this new model with other people, they were astonished by its effectiveness while in a conflict. They discovered that these are specific tools that can be used immediately in everyday life. Based on the feedback that I received, I developed workshops for people who want to learn to welcome conflict and for couples who want to work on it together. These skills, and the underlying theories, are the basis of The *Tell Me More Gesture*.

Workshop participants take the Gesture back to their own work environments, to their homes, and to their neighborhoods, and find that they can behave in a way during conflict that feels calm and wholesome and that leaves their dignity intact. People continue to practice the Gesture because of the peace of mind that it brings them. They experience less stress and they no longer fear difficult interactions.

We hear so often that people want deeper, more connecting lives— lives with meaning and purpose. We are looking to know more, understand more deeply, have interesting and thoughtful discussions, and go through hard times with people knowing that this is what makes relationships richer and more loving. The way to develop deeper, more connecting lives is to welcome conflict. The answer to how to welcome conflict is to learn the *Tell Me More Gesture*.

In this book you will find a variety of materials to help you deeply take in the information and develop the skills to begin your practice of welcoming conflict. I have included my own professional stories and personal anecdotes, exercises for practice, sections for journal entries, and quotes from a wide range of great thinkers to buoy you during reflective moments. This book is organized in a fashion for you to proceed through it chapter by chapter, step-by-step. By the end of the second chapter, you already will have tools to begin a new way of being with others who are upset. By the end of the book, you will have integrated new, positve habits in your everyday communication and be well on your way to establishing a practice of welcoming conflict.

I suggest that you try to not rush through the concepts in hopes of an immediate fix. Let the ideas linger as you do an exercise or journal entry; this will serve you well. You may want to take up the Gesture as an endeavor with a partner, trusted friend, or small discussion group. I offer a readers' forum at **tellmemoregesture.com.** I look forward to hearing from you as you progress through the book. I try to respond promptly to questions or struggles you may have. I am also pleased to hear stories of success or transformation.

Now, let's get started.

Chapter 1:
THE BIG SECRET
ABOUT CONFLICT

The words *fight or flight* often come to mind with the idea of conflict. Also, *compete*, *avoid*, *accommodate*, *compromise*, and *collaborate* are associated with conflict. You might have heard about finding win-win solutions. If you want to study and analyze conflict, all these ideas are useful. If you want to *do* something to help yourself deal with conflict in the most productive way possible, then continue on. Let's get to it.

> You cannot solve a problem from the same consciousness that created it. You must learn to see the world anew.
>
> —Albert Einstein,
> German-born theoretical physicist

The big secret about conflict is . . . [drumroll] . . . when people are upset, they *act* upset. You might think about it this way: When people experience conflict, they are likely to behave in ways that they do not normally behave when they are not in conflict. I immediately hear you thinking, *Really? That's it? Why is that so earth-shattering? That seems pretty darn obvious.*

Let's think about this: What do you consider to be good communication skills? When someone is upset, especially if they are upset with *you*, how do you expect them to behave? How should they communicate with you? I know at this point you're anxious to find out more, but before you continue, jot down a few words or phrases in the box below about how you expect this person to behave:

Exercise 1.1   When Someone Is Upset
[Duration: two minutes]

When someone is upset with me they should:

_____

_____

_____

_____

_____

_____

When I lead this exercise in workshops, here are some of the answers that participants give:

Exercise 1.1   When Someone Is Upset

Let's Try It Together

When someone is upset with me they should:

Be calm.	Listen.
Be respectful.	Be mature.
Be reasonable.	Be open.

This is the central theme that people express: When someone is upset they should be respectful and reasonable. They quote skills they have learned in couples' therapy, such as "avoid making accusations," "use 'I' statements," and "focus on the present." People sometimes say, "no blaming language" or "they should ask for what they need."

> He who knows one side of a thing, knows little of that.
>
> —African proverb

Interesting. As previously stated, when people are upset, they *act* upset. If this is true, why are we expecting distressed and angry people to be calm and reasonable? Is this a case of false expectations?

This question is not merely a rhetorical one. Why *do* we expect people to be calm and reasonable when they are upset? There are plenty of answers to this, and here are just a few: because conflict is difficult and messy; because we have been taught that conflict is bad; because conflict is not enjoyable; because in some cultures it is not socially acceptable to speak our minds; because sometimes being kind is more highly valued than being honest; because being disrespected doesn't feel good; and because it is easier to blame the other person for the manner in which they are speaking rather than take responsibility for our part.

How Do People Act When They Are Upset?

Now, think back to a time when someone was really upset with you. Think about who the person was and why they were so upset. (You may also have been very upset with them.) Think back to this time and remember how that person looked and how they acted. What was their behavior like? In the box below, use a few words or phrases to describe how that upset person appeared and behaved.

Exercise 1.2   How Someone Looks

[Duration: two minutes]

This is how someone looks and behaves when they are upset:

_____

_____

_____

_____

_____

_____

Did you come up with some words that ring true for you? You may have some negative feelings that come along with remembering and describing this person and this moment. These are not easy things to think about. Here are some answers from workshop participants:

Exercise 1.2 How Someone Looks

Let's Try It Together

This is how someone looks and behaves when they are upset:

Arrogant	Uncaring	Hateful
Unrelenting	Sad	Like a monster
Unreasonable	Angry	Irrational
Unaware	Blaming	Erratic
Shouting	Shut down	Selfish

What we notice is that generally people are not on their best behavior when they are upset. Many people intellectually understand how they are supposed to communicate and behave when they are upset, but once they are in the moment of distress, the good intention is not enough, and those skills go out the window.

Why is that? If we believe that the best way to communicate when we are upset is by using the skills we have learned in our quest for meaningful and evolved relationships, why aren't we using "I" statements, not bringing up the past, and asking for what we need, in voices that are calm and kind?

The shortest answer is this: We get triggered, flooded—call it what you want—but we lose capacity to be our best selves. Our brain chemistry changes when we are in conflict, and our capacity to respond calmly is extremely diminished. We start with good intentions and good communication skills, and then later, when things get tough, *boom*! We explode into all sorts of, let's say, emotional behavior. We lose the ability to do what our intellect knows it should do. Consider this story:

■   ■   ■

About a decade ago, I was a new member of a board of directors of a local, very small nonprofit company. Another new member, Grace, was outspoken, knowledgeable, an advocate of nonviolent communication, and progressive in her ideas. She convinced the board to change its method of operating from Robert's Rules of Order to consensus-based decision making. I was thrilled to learn about this inclusive way of operating and enjoyed the depth of discussions that arose from it. Just a couple of months later, we, as a board, were having a very difficult time coming to a decision regarding the executive director and his handling of staff matters. It had become a volatile issue and, at every board meeting, we kept getting hung up. After a few weeks of ongoing discussions, Grace stood firmly and alone in her stance on the issue, and the board could not move forward to make a decision. We were devoted to the consensus process, which forced us to work on it longer, and ideally more deeply. It appeared that no matter what we did, how much we listened, and how much Grace talked, nothing was changing.

Over the weeks, Grace was becoming more and more irritable, but we were managing to stay in the boundaries of the process. The truth is, Grace was holding the board hostage over a topic that was extremely important to her. Finally, after weeks of deliberating, we really pressured her to move on. We told her it was time for her to, at a minimum, give a neutral vote so that we could move forward. We recognized her opinion and would try to take that into consideration in the future. At this moment, Grace completely lost it. She started spewing f-bombs and directing insults at the board and at the process. This was shocking, of course. Here was an avid practitioner of nonviolent communication who, when push came to shove, behaved just like any person does when they are deep-down upset.

■   ■   ■

It is important to understand that the point is not to judge Grace for her behavior, but to truly appreciate that when people are upset, they *act* upset. We can actually expect the behavior. Utilizing any or all of the traditionally taught communication skills does not guarantee that our conversations will be successful.

The Universal Experience of Conflict

In Exercise 1.2 you thought about how someone looks and behaves when they are upset. Think back now to that same conflict. Think about yourself this time. Remember how the person treated you. How did you feel? Did you have any physical reaction? Please write a few words or phrases here about what you experienced:

Exercise 1.3   How I Feel
[Duration: two minutes]
This is how I feel when someone is acting upset at me:

How did that go? There are a wide range of emotions and sensations that are commonly mentioned here. I hope there is enough space for you! For comparison, here are some answers that others have come up with:

Exercise 1.3 How I Feel		

Let's Try It Together

This is how I feel when someone is acting upset at me:

Lost	Scared	Weak
Hopeless	Sad	Victimized
Anxious	Frustrated	Sick
Confused	Panicked	Invisible
Numb	Trapped	Incompetent

So what is the point of remembering back to these horrible times when we were experiencing conflict? Why is this relevant? Consider this: Is it possible that despite the behaviors we see on the outside of someone else, the anger, the blaming, the selfishness, on the inside the person might be feeling insecure, hopeless, and panicked? Is it possible that their actions are coming from their experience of being in conflict and not necessarily from them being a jerk?

The experience of being in conflict is fairly universal. According to the transformative theory of mediation, when people are in conflict, they are relatively weak and relatively self-absorbed compared to their normal selves.

Conflict, along with whatever else it does, affects people's experience of both self and other. First, conflict generates, for almost anyone it touches, a sense of their own weakness and incapacity . . . Conflict brings a sense of relative weakness, compared with their preconflict state, in their experience of self-efficacy: a sense of lost control over their situation, accompanied by confusion, doubt, uncertainty, and indecisiveness. This overall sense of weakening is something that occurs as a very natural human response to conflict; almost no one is immune to it regardless of his or her initial "power position." At the very same time, conflict generates a sense of self-absorption: compared with before, each party becomes more focused on self alone—more protective of self and more suspicious, hostile, closed, and impervious to the perspective of the other person. In sum, no matter how strong people are, conflict propels them into relative weakness. No matter how considerate of others people are, conflict propels them into self-absorption and self-centeredness (Bush and Folger 2005, 49).

As a result of this universal response to conflict, people get stuck in a conflict cycle that is negative, destructive, alienating, and demonizing (Bush and Folger 2005). While in a regular conversation we are able to consider the perspective of someone else. When we are in conflict we are necessarily more self-absorbed and therefore we are less likely to be able to do so. Therefore, we communicate in ways that are more defensive, more offensive, less rational, and less calm, compared to our normal selves.

In my mediator world, there are no jerks. There are only regular, lovely people who have arrived at a place where they can no longer act their best, and they are likely at this place for a very good reason. I do not need to know what that reason is. They do not have to prove to me in any way that they deserve to behave in ways that are considered ugly or out of line. I understand that when people are upset they *act* upset.

So my investigation began: If I can understand people this way in the mediation room, is this something that I can apply to myself when I have conflict with someone? Is there a way that I can withhold judgment about someone's demeaning or irrational behavior and see them as feeling hopeless and panicked, even when their upsetness is directed at me? Is there a way that I can reclaim the idea for my personal life that there are no jerks? I have discovered that yes, it is doable and extremely helpful.

How Do We Respond to Conflict?

Let's consider how we normally respond when someone is upset with us. Generally our responses fall into five types of behaviors.

> We must not seek happiness in peace, but in conflict.
>
> —Paul Claudel, French diplomat

1. We escalate.

We are indignant that someone is treating us disrespectfully so we up the ante—we do the same or worse. We lash out. We naturally try to protect ourselves and we do so by going on the offensive. This is a normal response. If we have a competitive nature, we might be even more likely to escalate when in conflict. Confrontation, threats, name-calling, put-downs, and physical demonstrations of our upsetness (hitting things, throwing things, etc.) all fall into this category. Obviously, if someone escalates the situation, while perhaps it is understandable, it is not a productive way to respond.

2. We defend.

There are a variety of ways that we defend ourselves when we are confronted with someone being upset at us.

The Misunderstanding Defense. We interrupt to say that there has been a misunderstanding. We believe that if we could get in a few words of rational thought, then they would calm down. In fact, there might not even be a problem at all if they would just listen for a second!

The I'm-Right-and-You're-Wrong Defense. Frequently, we are certain that we are right. We cut someone off because we know better. It is excruciating to listen to falsehoods, so we interrupt or talk over them, knowing that we are right. This is an end-justifies-the-means way of responding. We know it's not respectful to interrupt, but everything will get better faster if the upset person would just listen.

> What defeats us isn't the provocative speaker but our own defensive response.
>
> —Michael P. Nichols, *The Lost Art of Listening*

The I'm-Not-to-Blame Defense. Sometimes we give in to the urge to defend ourselves because we feel blamed or shamed—and getting blamed (or shamed) does not feel good. Defending ourselves feels like a way of protecting ourselves from the pain of this injustice. We need to tell why it happened, how it happened, or that it is absolutely not true that it happened. We believe we will be much more open to hearing what they have to say if we can first tell them that it is not our fault.

The Piling-On Defense. It often sounds like this: "I think you are wrong about this and you are also wrong about that thing and this other thing and you also did this to me one time and that to me another time." Or it might sound like this: "I think you are wrong, mistaken, or ridiculous and so does so-and-so," or even worse, "so does everyone else." This never feels good to hear, especially when one is upset and trying to communicate something important. It is tempting to use this method especially when you feel that you are not being believed. We think to ourselves, *If only they understood that I am not the only one who feels this way.* Making someone's faults into a universal experience also can be a slightly hidden method of escalating. It can be an I'm-hurt-so-I'm-going-to-hurt-you-worse type of response.

The bottom line is, being defensive is a method of shutting people down so that they will stop talking.

3. We fix.

We understand that there is a problem and if we can come up with a solution then the conflict will go away. We literally go into

> You can't see clearly through defensiveness.
>
> —Bryant McGill,
> *Simple Reminders*

> So whenever that brittle voice of dissatisfaction emerges within me, I can say "Ah, my ego! There you are, old friend!" It's the same thing when I'm being criticized and I notice myself reacting with outrage, heartache, or defensiveness. It's just my ego, flaring up and testing its power. In such circumstances, I have learned to watch my heated emotions carefully, but I try not to take them too seriously, because I know that it's merely my ego that has been wounded —never my soul.
>
> —Elizabeth Gilbert,
> *Big Magic*

problem-solving mode. However, if someone is upset and we start to generate ideas of how to help, we may not yet have heard the main points. We charge in with solid, rational ideas that will solve the speaker's distress and that can be put into action immediately.

Believe it or not, even an apology can be a way of trying to fix things. If an apology is offered while someone is still expounding, it often feels like an interruption and may not have the desired effect of communicating how sorry one is. Imagine someone saying, "I'm sorry, I'm sorry!" in the middle of your expressing how upset you are. The message to you is, "Stop talking and stop being upset because now everything should be fine."

An apology, even a very sincere one, can be a subtle attempt to fix the problem during conflict.

> Many a man would rather you heard his story than granted his request.
>
> —Phillip Stanhope,
> Earl of Chesterfield

Fixing is a commonly accepted way of responding to conflict. Everyone does it (including many mediators, who are supposedly experts at dealing with conflict).

It is often thought that *fixing* is exactly what is called for when people are upset: a cool head and creative problem solving; it is done in the spirit of helping someone to move forward. But fixing, although tempting (just ask my children), is rarely fruitful. When people are upset, it is absolutely another method of shutting them down. Fixing or problem solving is not helpful during conflict.

4. We shut down.

Silence is not always golden.

Sometimes when we are confronted with conflict, we avoid it. We shut down and either go silent or physically leave. Silence is not always golden. When we shut down

we are not open to information. We are not listening. We are
protecting ourselves by going inside an emotional shell.
We are desperate for relief from what might feel like a
barrage of insults and lies. We get relief by emotionally,
and sometimes physically, retreating. Shutting down
is another way of getting someone to stop talking. If
we are unavailable for the difficult conversation, there
is no conversation.

> Be leery of silence. It doesn't
> mean you won the argument.
> Often, people are just busy
> reloading their guns.
>
> —Shannon L. Alder,
> *American author*

5. We listen.

Sometimes we have the composure and patience to just listen. We
shut up and give the floor to the upset person. We let them vent,
understanding that if we allow them to get it out, they will calm down.
Hmm. Then why don't they always, or even usually, calm down? If
they do calm down, why do they get upset again? Venting may not
be as cathartic as we believe. Interestingly enough, one study says that
"venting to reduce anger is like using gasoline to put out a fire—it only
feeds the flame" (Bushman, 2). This brings into question how much
value there is in allowing someone to vent while we listen.

When we listen, we are silent. We completely give the
speaker the floor so that afterward we will receive, in
return, our opportunity to be heard. We are careful
not to interrupt. We sit in an observing manner trying
to hide any emotions we might be having so that we
do not distract the speaker. We are patiently waiting our
turn and we believe we are being good listeners. We might be getting

> **When you are not
> speaking, you are not
> necessarily listening.**

angrier and hotter as the time goes by. We would like to lash out, but we show restraint.

When we listen, we often are thinking ahead to what we will say when we finally get our turn. We stack up thoughts or write notes about what we will say when it is, finally, our turn. We are in essence being defensive, but we are not voicing these thoughts. What we are doing, actually, is pretending to listen. This is not listening.

> Most people do not listen with the intent to understand; they listen with the intent to reply.
>
> —Stephen R. Covey,
> *The 7 Habits of Highly Effective People*

Escalating, defending, fixing, shutting down, and pretending to listen: This is not an exhaustive list, nor a scientific study, of all the ways one might respond to conflict. What we are learning here though, is that we tend to respond in ways that, although understandable, are not productive. These behaviors do not welcome the conflict. We react in ways that attempt to shut down the person who is upset, and listening is often a guise for merely waiting out the storm. Now I hear you saying, "Listening? Even listening is not productive?"

Listening

OK, let's split hairs here. Sometimes listening is helpful. Sometimes if you are quiet and let the other person talk, they will indeed calm down, at least for the moment. Generally though, when a conflict is big enough or deep enough or emotional enough, shutting up and listening is not adequate. It will not resolve conflicts.

You will discover, as you read on through the next chapters, that the quality of the listening is important to the quality of the outcome of the conflict. In fact, it is so important that it is the crux of the matter in any conflict. In good conflict communication, you need to stop concentrating on the manner in which you speak and think more about how you listen. You need to stop trying to keep someone from acting upset and, in fact, expect it and welcome it. *What? Welcome "bad" behavior?* Yes, read on.

> **The quality of the listening is important to the quality of the outcome of a conflict.**

Moving Forward

We have discovered that when people are upset, they *act* upset. They are feeling and exhibiting characteristics of being relatively weak and self-absorbed compared to their normal selves. For many reasons, we tend not to welcome a discussion when someone is acting angry, not only because we have been socialized not to tolerate this behavior, but also because we, ourselves, are likewise in conflict and feeling weak and self-absorbed. So what is the right thing to do? Here we are, feeling stuck, alienated, and blamed. If escalating, defending, fixing, shutting down, and pretending to listen don't work, what does work?

The answer is for the participants to somehow (we will get to the *somehow* in the next chapter) speak and respond in ways that are beneficial. In transformative mediation terms, they return to a productive way of interacting. They move out of a communication cycle of weakness and self-absorption to feeling strong and responsive, to where the communication is one that is positive, constructive, connecting, and humanizing.

Conflict is not static. It is an emergent, dynamic phenomenon, in which parties can—and do—move and shift in remarkable ways, even when no third party is involved. They move out of weakness, becoming calmer, clearer, more confident, more articulate, and more decisive—in general, shifting from weakness to strength. They move away from self-absorption, becoming more attentive, open, trusting, and understanding of the other party—in general, shifting from self-centeredness to responsiveness to other (Bush and Folger 2005, 55).

So the question is: What can I do to change the cycle? What can I do to move from weakness to strength? What can I do to move from self-absorption to responsiveness? We need a new outlook. We need a new model. The answer is: Learn and practice the *Tell Me More Gesture*.

Before moving on to the next chapter, please take about fifteen minutes to reflect on and respond to the following journal questions. I encourage you to write down your answers in a paragraph or two for each entry. It will be useful for you to gather your responses here in the book so that you can refer back to them as you go through subsequent chapters. These exercises will help you absorb the information and practice new skills.

Journal Entry 1.1

When in conflict, are you most likely to escalate, defend, fix, or shut down? Do you have different responses in different situations? What are some examples? Why do you believe you react this (these) way(s)?

_____

_____

_____

_____

_____

_____

_____

_____

_____

_____

_____

_____

_____

_____

_____

_____

_____

_____

Journal Entry 1.2

When you are in listening mode, what attributes make you a good listener? Do you have any negative traits that accompany your listening? Do you have any positive or negative feelings associated with the topic of listening?

_____

_____

_____

_____

_____

_____

_____

_____

_____

_____

_____

_____

_____

_____

_____

_____

_____

_____

Chapter 2:
TELL ME MORE

Listening is something you do in a lecture; you listen intently to take in information, and to take it in deeply. Listening is something you do when you are waiting for a taxi, when you wait to hear the beep coming from outside, letting you know that it has arrived. You listen when you are out in nature, to identify the birdsong or to take in the sound of the water rushing over the rocks. You listen for pleasure or to gain knowledge or understanding.

> Nothing would astonish me, after all these years, except to be understood.
>
> —Ellen Glasgow, American novelist

This might be a shocking statement, but here it is: When in conflict, when someone is upset with you, listening is not the answer. It might be a better choice than going into fix-it mode or getting defensive, but listening is not the most productive thing to do. Here is the best thing to do: Lean forward and say, "Tell me more." That's it. That is the Gesture.

You must do both parts. You must physically lean forward toward the upset person and you must say, "Tell me more." When I tell this to workshop participants, I often receive blank looks in return. I have just told them, and now you, that literally in seven words, you can drastically alter the negative cycle that has begun, or that is about to begin. This is true.

> When people talk, listen completely. Most people never listen.
>
> —Ernest Hemingway, American novelist

There is certainly a lot more to learn about the Gesture–how to give nuance to it, how to make it your own, etc. But the basic gesture is indeed just these seven words: *lean forward and say tell me more.* This is a very important and initially awkward skill to integrate into your communication repertoire.

The idea of leaning forward can be an uncomfortable notion. When you hear something such as, "You're a lazy slob," or "You never listen to me," or "You only think of yourself," your first impulse is most likely to recoil from the attacking statements. Even if you are not physically recoiling, you are likely trying to maintain your composure in order to remain sitting there. The thing to do is to lean toward the person who is saying those awful things (seriously!) and say, "Tell me more." I'm going to ask you to go on blind faith for now and just give it a try. Before we go any further into the explanations and skill building, please do the following two quick exercises.

Exercise 2.1   Just Say It

[Duration: fifteen seconds]

Say aloud five times:

TELL ME MORE.

(Seriously, do it.)

These words must roll off your tongue very easily.

Now try this:

Exercise 2.2   In the Looking Glass

[Duration: two minutes]

1. Go to a mirror.
2. Look into your own eyes, lean forward, and say, "Tell me more."
3. Do you believe it? Did you actually lean forward?
4. Say it several more times to yourself in the mirror until you can do it without giggling and until you demonstrate that you do indeed want to know more.

Now that you are comfortably saying, "Tell me more," you should know that what you are actually doing is _giving someone the feeling of getting listened to_. This is very different from listening and is actually much more than listening. Mastering this Gesture will change your interactions with people for the better. The key is to recognize that real listening is not just shutting up and waiting for the speaker to be finished. It requires

> We listen in order to understand. We say, "Tell me more," so that the speaker can feel listened to. These are very different.

you to prove to the speaker that you are engaged. You will find that giving someone the feeling of getting listened to is useful not only in conflict, but also in regular situations when someone is merely telling you a story about their day or about their conflict with someone else.

I should admit this to you: I am not naturally a good listener. I have too much to say, too many ideas, and I get on a roll and start repeating myself. I am an extrovert in almost every way. I get energy from being around people. I am an out-loud processor. Learning to give people the feeling of getting listened to, and practicing it in my personal life, has helped me understand that I can be very satisfied saying less. I have grown immeasurably from practicing the *Tell Me More Gesture*.

> Man's inability to communicate is a result of his failure to listen effectively.
>
> —Carl Rogers, American psychologist

I have learned that people come forward with important things to say when I accomplish this encouraging gesture. The Gesture demonstrates that I believe in their inherent worth. I have also learned that when I do not do this, when I react defensively or lash out or go into fix-it mode, it is a way of demeaning them, as if they are not equal to me. This realization shocked me. I believe that we are all equal—that we all matter. Making room for others to speak, and making sure that I give them the feeling of getting listened to, allows me to live to my values. This has been a personal transformation, although it is an ongoing practice.

I want you to understand this about me because it might appear that the Gesture is most suitable for people who are introverts or naturally Zen. I have seen many types of people have great success and satisfaction from the Gesture. Extroverts, introverts, people who use their intuition, people who like facts, people who are emotional, people who are logical—this model works well for all types because, as discussed in chapter 1, our need for connection is universal. The Gesture allows connection to be maintained or restored between people during very difficult interactions.

Before moving on to learning more about the Gesture, it is important that you practice leaning forward and saying, "Tell me more." I have led many workshops and have come to realize that while this looks easy, it is indeed hard to do when faced with a difficult conversation. Please do the following exercise before moving on to the next section.

> I define connection as the energy that exists between people when they feel seen, heard, and valued; when they can give and receive without judgment; and when they derive sustenance and strength from the relationship.
>
> —Brené Brown,
> *The Gifts of Imperfection*

Exercise 2.3   You're a Jerk!

[Duration: five minutes]

You will need another person's help for this exercise. This is usually fun for both of you. For more practice, try this exercise with several different people.

1. Write down five horrible statements that you would hate to hear from someone. Or you may use these:
   - You're a jerk!
   - You're as bad as your father!
   - You're a flaming narcissist!
   - You never listen to me!
   - How could you be so stupid?
2. Ask your person to say these to you, one at a time, with a lot of feeling. They could even yell at you.
3. After each statement, pause for just a second, then lean forward and say, "Tell me more," as if you truly want to hear more.
4. Ask your person how that felt. Did they feel encouraged to say more? Did they feel like you would be genuinely interested?

Perhaps this exercise feels awkward. Encouraging a person to say unkind things is likely counterintuitive. Notice that part of the exercise is to determine if your person actually felt like you wanted to hear more. This is the true test because, remember, the whole idea of the Gesture is to give the upset speaker the feeling of getting listened to.

It can be tempting to put a different spin on the "tell me more" statement and use sarcasm or make a motion or an eye roll to let the speaker know that you have feelings about what was said. Don't do it. Or at times you may start to giggle; don't worry about that. It is a little uncomfortable at first, but keep practicing. Start over and do it until you can sincerely demonstrate your encouragement for them to say more.

Believe it or not, these words, "Tell me more," along with leaning forward, will make a huge improvement in your communication during conflict. There are other things that you can say, but when push comes to shove, you can always say, "Tell me more." Check out the following two stories:

■   ■   ■

Katy was a workshop attendee who, during an exercise, had a hard time saying, "Tell me more," without feeling phony. She felt sheepish about trying to make it sound real and, in fact, her words had a sarcastic tone. We discussed that, especially at first, the authenticity is in the sincerity of trying this new model. Katy felt free then to keep trying the method, even if it felt strange. The very next day after the workshop, I received a note from Katy telling me that she had given it a try at home. She and her husband had taken a walk, and he had started talking to her in a way to which she normally would have had a bad reaction. He had told her she was being dense. Instead of reacting to this slight, she used the exact words, "Tell me more." Katy reported that the conversation went in a completely different direction from what she had ever previously experienced. She reported feeling good about herself for being able to do this. Her husband, when invited

> The Gesture may feel awkward at first. The authenticity is in the sincerity of trying.

to say more, not only did say more but also changed his tone and got clear on what was really bothering him.

■ ■ ■

Being genuine is very important to people, and feeling less-than-authentic with this new skill is a common frustration. You cannot be sarcastic or act uninterested and just say the words. This is not the Gesture. You must practice it so that the speaker can feel your good intentions. Take a leap of faith that something good will come with this new skill.

Here is a story about Dorothy, a great example of how to creatively utilize the statement, even if you haven't had a lot of practice.

■ ■ ■

Dorothy never had children, but enjoyed helping out at her niece's home. Her niece's children felt like her own grandchildren, and she was fortunate to see them often. Since her niece and husband went off to work extremely early, Dorothy was at their home some mornings to get the children off to school. Regardless of who was in charge, the routine in their home was for ten-year-old Joe to put up a big fuss about having to practice the piano. He would complain and give excuses. The adult was to hear nothing of it because it was merely a way of Joe getting out of his full thirty-minute practice. Dorothy didn't enjoy being in the position of carrying out this unpleasant routine, but she felt she needed to follow her niece's wishes and would do everything she could to make sure Joe practiced the required time.

Soon after our workshop together, Dorothy was at their house and about to go through the same discord, which she detested. Joe had started complaining about his practice time. Instead of giving him the hand motion to just go do it, Dorothy sat down on the floor with him and simply said, "Joe, tell me more." In fact, Joe did tell her more. Joe told her about his dislike of the piece that he was supposed to practice and about how he was tired of getting up extra early to practice. Dorothy withheld the impulse to defend why he was to practice. She didn't tell him how gifted he was. She didn't tell him that he would understand when he was older. She made sure that Joe felt listened to. Within a few minutes, Joe was playing a different piece at the piano to show off for his dear auntie, which was the beginning of a lovely, albeit shortened, practice session.

■   ■   ■

Dorothy used the Gesture in an unexpected way. She was not being personally attacked, yet she used the skill to promote a positive interaction during a difficult time. This is a good example of how the Gesture can be used for what is the equivalent of a one-way conversation (chapter 3). Dorothy had let go of any expectation of getting heard. She instead decided to give Joe the feeling of getting listened to. With the small statement of "Tell me more," she changed the unpleasant pattern into a positive and connecting experience.

Even under the time pressure of having to get the practicing accomplished before school, Dorothy stayed focused on Joe getting heard.

Dorothy's actions were an inspiration to me. Being patient when the clock is ticking is difficult for me. When I feel time pressure, whether it is helping with homework, driving to an appointment, or meeting friends for dinner, I can have a very short fuse. I learned from Dorothy that I can let time go in order to be in the moment with whoever needs to get heard. Most anything can wait, and I likely save time by listening longer; when the conversation remains productive, it often concludes faster.

> There's a lot of difference between listening and hearing.
>
> —G. K. Chesterton, English writer

Safety Net Phrases

"Tell me more" is a great fallback statement and is just the tip of the iceberg in terms of ways that you can help someone feel listened to. When someone attacks with a hostile or inflammatory statement, we are likely to lash out in return or to tell them to restate what they are trying to say in a kinder manner. When we are feeling attacked, we tend to be shocked at first, inarticulate and awkward, so it is important to rely on "tell me more" as a safety net.

There are a couple other *safety net phrases* that I use quite often. I use them because they feel good to the speaker when they are upset and because, whichever one I choose, it is true for me in the moment. I am being completely authentic, even though I utilize the same phrases time and time again. Here they are:

SAFETY NET PHRASES

1. Tell me more. (or) Is there more?
2. You've had it!
3. This is really hard, but I'm going to keep trying.

These are phrases that you may use to reflect back the essence of what you are hearing from the upset person. Here is an example of a conversation where the listener is using only the *safety net phrases*:

SPEAKER: "You're a jerk!"

LISTENER: [leaning forward] "Wow, you've had it!"

SPEAKER: "Yes, I've had it! You've made me wait for you for the very last time. I'm not going through this anymore."

LISTENER: [leaning forward] "Tell me more."

SPEAKER: "You're always late. I feel humiliated waiting for you for forty-five minutes. I've been sitting at this table all by myself. The server keeps asking me if I want to order. You're completely self-centered. You only think of yourself."

LISTENER: "OK. This is really hard, but I'm going to keep trying." [leaning forward] "Is there more?"

SPEAKER: "Yes, there's more!"

[And so on.]

This is the beginning of a successful interaction because the speaker not only has the opportunity to get heard, but also feels the genuine interest of the listener. Notice that the speaker gets more upset and the listener is not trying to avoid this. Remember, the essence of the *Tell Me More Gesture* is to welcome difficult discussions.

The following exercise will give you good practice in beginning the Gesture. You do not have a lot of tools yet and you may feel hesitant at first, but you will be surprised by how well you can do with just the *safety net phrases*. Please use only these phrases during this conversation. Make sure that you are not merely silent. You will not defend or fix; you will only give the feeling of getting listened to. This is a one-way conversation. This means you listen with no expectation of getting listened to in return.

I am happiest when I do what I am afraid to do.

—William Moyers,
Broken

Exercise 2.4   Welcoming Conflict

[Duration: ten minutes each]

Conduct a short conversation where you welcome a difficult topic. Do this with three different people in the following manner:

1. Find someone to agree to be a guinea pig for this new conflict communication work you are doing.

2. Tell this person that you want to listen to them—that you want them to tell you something difficult. If you prefer, you could ask them to choose something not too difficult for this beginning exercise. Also tell them that you do not expect to have your say—you just want them to have the opportunity to get listened to.

3. Using only the three *safety net phrases*, do your best to give this person the feeling of getting listened to. When you have the impulse to defend yourself or offer a solution, just say, "Tell me more." For your reference, here are the *safety net phrases*:

   1. Tell me more.
   2. You've had it!
   3. This is really hard, but I'm going to keep trying.

4. When you believe the person is done, ask them, "Do you feel done?" If they say "No," then you say, "OK, please tell me more." If they say "Yes," then thank them and ask them the following questions: "How did that feel for you?" "Was this more or less rewarding than the way we normally discuss difficult things?" You are determining if they feel satisfied (even though the conversation is a little awkward because you do not yet have many new skills yet).

5. Notice how you feel while you are doing the exercise. Use journal entry 2.2 at the end of this chapter as a guide for your reflection.

Giving Recognition

As you know by now, it is important to differentiate between *listening* and *the feeling of getting listened to.* You are the listener in both instances, but listening is just a portion of what you are doing. Listening focuses on you as the listener, that is, whether or not *you* hear and whether *you* understand, while giving the feeling of getting listened to focuses on the speaker, that is, what is happening for them while you are listening. One descriptive term for this is *giving recognition* because it refers to giving (the feeling) rather than receiving (information). "Giving the feeling of getting listened to" could also be called *giving satisfaction.*

> Giving that is genuine and freely chosen can bring us enduring inner satisfaction, precisely because it meets our deepest need to be useful and connected to others, because it allows us to make a difference in the world of others, and because it just makes us feel good. Paradoxically, it is by giving that we often receive what we most want.
>
> —William Ury,
> *Getting to Yes with Yourself*

Notice that when you are attentive in this way you are also more likely to achieve a deeper understanding, even though your primary goal is on giving recognition rather than receiving information. It is also important to note that we cannot control the speaker. We cannot ensure that someone will feel listened to or feel satisfied, but our goal remains to do so.

There is nothing in this Gesture that tells the speaker that you agree or disagree, nor that you approve or disapprove, nor that you are enjoying or disliking the process. This is not the time to send signals about your feelings. Giving recognition gives no message about the listener except that you are engaged, that you are trying to understand, and that you care.

Five Listening Styles

Becoming a skillful, responsive listener is the beginning of being proficient at the *Tell Me More Gesture*. Often we receive advice from people, from books, from seminars that simply say, "Listen more," but not everyone understands what this means. Demonstrating that one is truly listening is an art. As children we are taught to talk, but are we taught how to listen?

In this section, we examine the skill of listening with the purpose of determining how productive it is for the speaker. Our behavior as the listener gives indications to the speaker about three things: our interest, our comprehension, and how much we care. That is, the level of engagement demonstrated by the listener indicates their level of interest in the topic, comprehension of the topic, and connection to the speaker.

> Listening is a gift of spiritual significance that you can learn to give to others ... When you listen, you give one a sense of importance, hope and love that he or she may not receive any other way. Through listening, we nurture and validate the feelings one has, especially when he or she experiences difficulties in life.
>
> —H. Norman Wright,
> *Recovering from Losses in Life*

Five Listening Styles

1. **Bored/distracted listening**
   Level of Engagement: This is scarcely listening. In general, this type of listener has a minimum amount of eye contact and might be fidgeting or shuffling things. They might be looking around, checking the clock or their cell phone. They might be asking questions that are off-topic or changing the topic.

Outcome: This type of listening indicates to the speaker that the listener has:

- A low level of interest
- A low level of comprehension
- A low level of connection

This style of listening gives the message to the speaker that the listener has no desire to be present and, virtually, is not present.

2. Detached listening

Level of Engagement: Detached listening creates an invisible boundary between the speaker and the listener. This might also be called doubtful listening. This listener might have a bit of eye contact, but they are sitting back in their chair, there are few visible actions or reactions, and their arms might be folded in front of them. They are likely making few reflections and asking few questions.

> Detached listening creates an invisible boundary between the speaker and the listener.

Outcome: This style of listening indicates to the speaker that the listener has:

- A moderate amount of interest
- A moderate amount of comprehension
- A low amount of connection

Detached listening is an improvement over distracted listening, but it is clear that the listener does not care about the situation and/or about the speaker.

3. **Defensive listening**

    Level of Engagement: The defensive listener might have high energy, but often the energy is accompanied by a low level of eye contact. There is likely gesturing, interrupting, and sometimes feverish note taking. There may be defensive listeners who are silent, but inside they are thinking of ways to combat or explain away the speaker's statements.

    Outcome: The speaker understands that the defensive listener has:
    *   A high level of interest
    *   A low level of comprehension
    *   A low level of connection

    This type of listening is similar to bored/distracted listening—the listener is more concerned with self than with listening to the message from the speaker.

4. **Observant listening**

    Level of Engagement: The observant listener likely gives the speaker a moderate amount of eye contact and is sitting up straight demonstrating attention. This listener makes neutral-sounding reflections and asks neutral-sounding questions to ensure good comprehension.

    Outcome: The speaker understands that the observant listener has:
    *   A moderate amount of interest
    *   A moderate amount of comprehension
    *   A moderate amount of connection

Observant listening is often used in the mediation and legal fields, as well as in other helping professions. It is intended to keep a boundary between the consultant and the client. Observant listening is also utilized as a technique to disengage, yet still remain present. This type of listening often has a feel of judgment or superiority due to the listener having a neutral affect during a heated discussion. Observant listening can prevent the speaker from feeling completely understood and diminishes the likelihood of a good outcome because it purposefully undermines the connection between the speaker and listener.

> He did it (listened) as the world's more charming and magnetic people do, always asking the right question at the right time, never fidgeting or taking his eyes from the speaker's face, making the other guy feel like the most knowledgeable, brilliant, and intellectually savvy person on the planet.
>
> —Stephen King,
> *11/22/63*

5. **Empathic listening**

   Level of Engagement: The empathic listener generally has a high amount of eye contact with the speaker (or as much as is comfortable for the speaker). The listener is likely sitting forward, nodding, and making reflections that include any apparent emotion. In general, the empathic listener has a kind and accepting facial expression.

   Outcome: The speaker understands that the empathic listener has:
   - A high level of interest
   - A high level of comprehension
   - A high level of connection

   The speaker generally feels some amount of comfort from being with the empathic listener. The speaker feels accepted, not judged. Notice that there is no indication that the listener agrees with the speaker. People are sometimes hesitant to nod or show understanding, concerned that it will be misconstrued as agreement. This is a common misconception. There is a distinct and perceptible difference between nodding to show agreement and nodding to show interest. Not everyone who is an empathic listener nods as they are listening. They might be leaning forward with their head tilted. Their eyes might have a bright intensity. There are many ways to be an empathic listener.

This listening styles comparison demonstrates that that the listener has a lot of control over the quality of the conversation. Our conduct demonstrates our intention to give recognition to the speaker—to help the speaker feel satisfied and valued. Feeling valuable is important at any time, but even more significant when one is in conflict. Imagine if when you were upset, someone listened to you as if you were an asset—as if you were valuable. Wonderful!

> **The listener has a lot of control over the quality of the conversation.**

Moving Forward

Chapter 2 has introduced the first basic principle of the *Tell Me More Gesture*: You must not merely listen; you must give the speaker the feeling of getting listened to. You now understand that you need to lean forward when you are listening during a conflict, and you need to say encouraging statements that demonstrate your interest, your understanding, and

> People need to feel valuable. We need this almost as we need food, air, and water. It's not good enough for us to know in our own hearts that we're valuable; we need to see our worth reflected in the eyes of the people around us.
>
> —Mark Goulston, *Just Listen*

that you care. You have learned and practiced the three *safety net phrases* that help you accomplish this. You now understand that you have a lot of power to change the quality of a conflict conversation (or any conversation) merely by improving the manner in which you listen. Please spend ten to fifteen minutes completing the following journal entries, where you can reflect on what you have learned so far.

When we are listened to, it creates us, makes us unfold and expand. Ideas actually begin to grow within us and come to life.

—Brenda Ueland,
Strength To Your Sword Arm

Journal Entry 2.1

Using only the *safety net phrases* in conflict conversations can feel limiting, but it is good practice when you are just beginning to learn the *Tell Me More Gesture*. When you were using the *safety net phrases*, what other questions or statements were you tempted to use?

_____

_____

_____

_____

_____

_____

_____

_____

_____

_____

_____

_____

_____

_____

_____

_____

_____

_____

_____

_____

_____

Journal Entry 2.2

In Exercise 2.4 (page 37), as you were practicing giving the speaker the feeling of getting listened to, what feelings in your self did you notice? What worked well? What were your frustrations? Was it easier or more difficult than you anticipated?

_____

_____

_____

_____

_____

_____

_____

_____

_____

_____

_____

_____

_____

_____

_____

Chapter 3:
THE ONE-WAY CONVERSATION

By now you understand well that the first key tenet of the *Tell Me More Gesture* is to give someone the feeling of getting listened to. We have discussed that this can be called giving recognition and that it must not only be given, it must also be received and felt by the speaker, or we have not truly accomplished the Gesture. We do not have control over the speaker being able to feel the Gesture, but it is nevertheless the goal.

> Listening, not talking, is the gifted and great role, and the imaginative role. And the true listener is much more believed, magnetic than the talker, and he is more effective and learns more and does more good.
>
> —Brenda Ueland,
> *Strength To Your Sword Arm*

The second key part to the Gesture is that you must do this until the speaker is all-the-way done. This is a one-way conversation, at least temporarily, with no expectation by the listener of getting heard. We throw away expectations, knowing that we can be the best listener if we are not inhibited by our own needs for getting heard, by feeling like a victim, or even by defending our position inside our own head.

Listening until someone is all-the-way done is very similar to wringing out a washcloth. You begin by giving someone who is upset at you the feeling of getting listened to. Although it is not pleasant and it is not easy, you lean forward and you say, "Tell me more." They evidently have more to say, so you keep going, you keep giving recognition. You are wringing the washcloth again and again.

You make reflections (see chapters 4 and 5) so that they can feel listened to. They feel acknowledged. The washcloth is drier, but still it is holding water. They might calm down, yet still have even more to say. You keep leaning forward. You let them know that you still want to hear more. This continues until they have no more to tell you, until the washcloth has no more water to release. Sometimes they think they are done and then, when you begin to talk, they interrupt you and start talking again. They weren't really done. So, this is still an opportunity to go back to being the listener, if you can manage it. You change your role and your mentality from speaker to listener.

> An appreciative listener is always stimulating.
>
> —Agatha Christie,
> *The Mysterious Affair at Styles*

■ ■ ■

A few years ago, a married couple, Betty and Brad, were in my office. They had been together for decades and wanted to discuss some difficult matters, both logistical issues and harms done. They also wanted training on how to go through conflict more productively. Betty, the person who was most visibly upset, spent the first few sessions doing most of the speaking, and I helped Brad be a listener so that Betty could feel listened to. This was very hard work, but both participants felt it was very worthwhile. One week it became apparent that the roles needed to be reversed. Betty, who had previously felt too victimized by their conflict to even consider being able to listen to Brad, was ready to do the *Tell Me More Gesture* with Brad. As they arrived for the session, it was clear by Betty's open expression and relaxed body language that she was up for the one-way conversation. Brad spent the full hour and a half being the speaker, and Betty did a very good job of listening to difficult information and still giving Brad the feeling of getting listened to. At the end of the session, she checked in with Brad to see if the session had been satisfactory for him and, indeed, it had. I checked in with Betty about how it had gone for her. She looked at me, tilted her head, and said, "I don't even know! I was so taken with the listening part and wasn't thinking about myself at all!"

■ ■ ■

Bingo! Betty had completely given herself over to giving recognition to Brad. Even when things were very hard to hear, Betty had found a way to find empathy for Brad, even if she had been, according to Brad, the cause of his grief. Betty would not get listened to in a reciprocal way until the next session, yet she felt satisfied and buoyed by her ability to accomplish this difficult task and by the connection that she felt to Brad.

Before reading on, complete Exercise 3.1. You will complete the exercise once, then you will understand that it will be advantageous to practice it many times

> And Edward was surprised to discover that he was listening. Before, when Abilene had talked to him, everything had seemed so boring, so pointless. But now, the stories Nellie told struck him as the most important thing in the world and he listened as if his life depended on what she said.
>
> —Kate DiCamillo,
> *The Miraculous Journey of Edward Tulane*

in your everyday conversations. This will help you prepare to use the Gesture when there is conflict. Exercise 3.1 can be used during most any daily conversation. When someone, for example, is explaining what happened on the subway, how they got into a car accident, or about a conversation they had with their boss—when someone is telling you a story of any kind—this is a very good opportunity to practice briefly turning it into a one-way conversation.

Exercise 3.1   The One-Way Conversation

[Duration: a few minutes]

1. As someone tells you a story about their day, remember that you want to practice the *Tell Me More Gesture*. Remembering, or finding the impulse, is always the first step.

2. As you hear the story, give the speaker the feeling of getting listened to by saying, "Tell me more." Even if the topic or person normally bores you, your interest is in giving recognition to them. You may find that a topic becomes more interesting when you stay engaged in this manner.

3. Be certain that you listen longer than you normally would; try extending the conversation past where the topic would normally drop.

4. Note any changes in the speaker's behavior in Journal Entry 3.1. Do they seem buoyed by your extra interest? Do they talk more in depth as well as longer? Do their speech patterns change? Does their mood lighten or get more intense? Do you find out more than you would have if you had done a normal style of listening? Did you feel more interested as the time went by? Did you enjoy the listening more or less than you would have otherwise?

Now that you have practiced the Gesture during nonconflict conversations, you will find it more natural to do so during a difficult conversation. Please know that, when using the *Tell Me More Gesture* during a conflict, each of us has our limit. We are human. Everyone has hot buttons, hurdles, and triggers (see chapter 8) as they are learning to give someone the feeling of getting listened to and doing it until the speaker is all-the-way done. Also know that most everyone can exceed their limit. You can go longer and do better than you imagined. And when you do this, you should know that you are the beneficiary.

Ten Gifts for You, the Listener

When someone is angry at you, and perhaps using rough and accusatory language, you are likely not in the mood for giving them a gift, in this case, the gift of giving them recognition. It is imperative that you understand that this is not merely a gift for the speaker, and it is not you subordinating yourself so that someone else can feel lifted up. While there are many benefits to the speaker from feeling listened to and from getting heard until they are finished, the benefits to the listener are numerous.

> When you talk, you are only repeating what you already know. But if you listen, you may learn something new.
>
> —Dalai Lama,
> *Tibetan Buddhist monk*

o o o

The Ten Gifts of Listening

Gift #1: Slow down. The first thing that listening does is it allows you to slow down. Slowing down prevents you from feeling you need to respond quickly. Slowing down gives you the space to relax and not feel the pressure, nor the temptation, to respond.

Gift #2: Calm down. Listening gives you the time to calm down. While you are giving someone the feeling of getting listened to, you could also be managing your breathing or letting your neck and shoulders relax.

Gift #3: Learn. Giving someone the feeling of getting listened to almost ensures that you will learn something. You will open yourself to understanding that the speaker may have good points and a valid perspective, and you will find out more about the speaker as a person, and about yourself.

Gift #4: Get clear. Listening will allow you to gain clarity, organize details, and feel less chaotic. When you accomplish the Gesture, you will find that you are able to make sense of someone else's way of thinking, even if you disagree.

Gift #5: Reduce stress. When you are able to slow down, calm down, and feel empowered, you are naturally reducing your stress. In addition, you have the benefit of not anticipating and fearing conflict, which is a common source of everyday stress.

Gift #6: Engage. One of the best attributes of the *Tell Me More Gesture* is that it will help you stay engaged. During conflict it is common to begin to shut down and not truly listen. Giving someone the feeling of getting listened to forces you to stay present and receptive to the speaker.

Gift #7: Feel empowered. Giving recognition to the speaker is an empowering gesture for the listener. It helps you feel strong and self-reliant and leaves you with an overall feeling of self-respect and accomplishment.

Gift #8: Go deeper. Giving someone the feeling of being listened to and doing it until they are all the way done is a productive path for going through conflict. Relationships gain deeper understanding from going through difficult experiences together.

Gift #9: Feel connected. In the end, using the Gesture allows you to feel connected to your partner, a relative, a friend, a work associate, a neighbor, a shopkeeper, or even a stranger. Feeling connected during and after difficult discussions is exactly what we are striving for. This is an incredible gift to ourselves because we don't abandon our own need for connection during times of conflict.

Gift #10: Live to your values. What are your values? Honesty? Kindness? Respect? Fairness? Transparency? Integrity? Giving recognition to the speaker, during times of conflict as well as during normal conversation, is an opportunity for you to live to your values.

The Gesture is an opportunity for you to help yourself in times of conflict, which appears to be self-sacrificing but is actually self-serving when you consider all of the gifts it brings to you. You may find that there are other benefits to you that have not been mentioned here.

> Listening is being able to be changed by the other person.
>
> —Alan Alda, American Actor

Thinking back to the story of Betty and Brad (page 39), Betty's extreme satisfaction at the end of her listening tenure was a result of her feeling self-respect and personal success (Gift #7) in accomplishing the Gesture and her ability to maintain connection (Gift #9) with Brad while he was saying difficult things. She may, of course, also have learned things (Gift #3), and it may ultimately deepen their relationship (Gift #8) from going through even just this portion of their difficulty in this productive manner. It serves the listener both as an individual and as a person needing to be connected to others.

Check out the following story about Lori and Douglas. Lori was working on being the listener and received an unexpected gift as a result of practicing the Gesture.

■ ■ ■

Lori and Douglas, together thirteen years and never married, arrived at my office for a two-hour, private workshop, with Douglas walking about five paces behind Lori. By the last half hour of the session, Douglas, the introvert of the two, was much more believable when he was practicing the Gesture with Lori. It was evident that he really meant it when he asked Lori to tell him more. Lori agreed that she was struggling with being the listener. It felt awkward. We discussed that it is common to not want to appear inauthentic. The authenticity is in the act of trying. We have to practice reflecting with a heartfelt attitude and manner. If the speaker can't feel that the listener is interested and open to more information, then the reflection is not as worthwhile and may, in fact, backfire and appear mimicking and belittling.

So I asked Lori to try her reflection again with the same words. Before she began I asked her if she could relax her shoulders. She did so, and I was amazed by how far they lowered. And I asked her to put her hands in her lap, which she did comfortably. And I reminded her to lean forward a bit. Then Douglas restated the (purposefully) rude statement that they were using for practice, "Use your head, Lori! If we just do these things, it'll be fine!"

Lori leaned toward him, looked right at him, and said, "It's going to be just fine! Tell me more." Their eyes stayed on each other, and Lori's eyes teared up a bit.

"I believed you, Lori. I felt that," he told her. A few tears came. As Lori dabbed her eyes, she told us that the act of lowering her shoulders somehow had made her feel vulnerable, less protected. Douglas was very touched by this. He told her how happy he was to see this side of her again. He admitted to me that she had dragged him to this private workshop today, and that he had given up going on a big motorcycle ride to do so. He was grateful that they had come and as he looked at Lori, her face was still soft and open.

■ ■ ■

Lori had experienced the gift of staying engaged (Gift #6). When she left herself open, she was able to experience closeness and connection (Gift #9) even though she was upset. Remaining vulnerable when faced with conflict is extremely difficult, and may take a lot of practice, but it is also a shortcut to finding peace with each other.

Conflict Mantra Cards

In order for the Gesture to work for you, you must deeply understand your own motivation because this is what will keep you on track in the times of heated conflict. The *Tell Me More Gesture* helps maintain connection between the speaker and the listener during a conflict and therefore, because we are relational beings, both participants have the likelihood of experiencing a fulfilling exchange. Even listeners who do not get the reciprocal experience of being listened to report increased satisfaction with their communication.

> Intention functions not only as a starting point but also as an anchor when we become confused or disoriented in our communications.
>
> —Diane Musho Hamilton, *Everything Is Workable*

We are not expecting people to be able to be calm and rational, because we know what it feels like to be in distress. Thích Nhất Hanh, a Vietnamese Buddhist monk and peace advocate, names one's distress as suffering. He says that we should listen with only one intention: to help the speaker suffer less (Hanh 2013). This idea of helping the other person suffer less is exceptional, but it must be balanced with the deep understanding that the Gesture is equally a gift to the listener.

The following exercise is an effective way for you to be mindful of your intention. Why are you learning the Gesture?

> And the day came when the risk to remain tight in a bud was more painful than the risk it took to blossom.
>
> —Anaïs Nin,
> French memoirist & feminist

Exercise 3.2   Conflict Mantra Cards

[Duration: fifteen minutes]

1. Look back at the *Ten Gifts of Listening* on pages 52-53, and find the *one* most compelling reason for you to listen to someone when they are being unkind to you. Be honest with yourself about what really motivates you to try out the Gesture. You are welcome to change the wording or create something completely new. This is *your* conflict mantra.

2. Make three copies of the conflict mantra card (below) and cut them out. If you have cardstock or thick paper, the card will last longer—or design your own card with the same prompts. You may also print the cards from the Readers' Forum at tellmemoregesture.com.

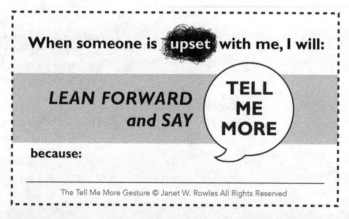

When someone is upset with me, I will:

LEAN FORWARD and SAY   TELL ME MORE

because:

_____

3. On the line below "because," write your conflict mantra. There are examples of others' cards on the next page. Write the *same mantra* on all three cards. You may do more cards, if you wish.

4. Place the three (or more) cards in locations where you will view them often. It is up to you if you want to keep them in places that are more private, such as in your wallet, in the top drawer of your desk, or in a drawer in your bathroom, or more public, such as on the refrigerator, on your mirror in the bathroom, on your car dashboard, or on your computer at work.

5. Whenever you see your mantra card, read it out loud to yourself. Ideally you will say it twenty times a day or more.

EXAMPLES OF MANTRA CARDS

My own mantra card is the first example on the previous page. I read it aloud like this: "When someone is upset with me, I will lean forward and say, 'Tell me more,' because it is important for me to live to my values." This is my truth. If I treat someone badly, lashing out or interrupting, I might feel entitled and empowered in the moment. Lashing out is like a drug high or a sugar buzz; it feels like a good idea in the moment. But after the drug has worn off, after the moment is over and I am more in control, the high disappears, the entitlement fades, and I feel extremely sad and low. I am motivated to eliminate such grief and depletion from my life. When I live to my values, when I don't lash out or interrupt, it means I don't have to feel bad about myself. Your conflict mantra should have deep meaning for you. Having the self-awareness about how it will benefit you is crucial to your success with the *Tell Me More Gesture*.

Contemplative Silence

By now you understand that there are two core aspects to the *Tell Me More Gesture*:

1. Give the feeling of getting listened to, and
2. Continue until the speaker is all-the-way done.

There is one more important part to the success of the Gesture which occurs *after* the Gesture is complete:

3. Reserve time for contemplative silence.

Contemplative silence is a time after the speaker is finished for both the speaker and listener to think about what has happened so far. Up until this point, you have been listening intently and giving recognition to the speaker. You have not let in thoughts about how to respond because that would detract from the Gesture. You have not worried about defending yourself because you know there will be time, after the speaker is done, for you to collect your thoughts.

> Judicious silences are important in any work.
>
> —Claude Debussy, French composer

Contemplative silence is time intentionally set aside for you to do just that. Now you have time to reflect. How are you doing? What feelings have come up since the speaker began? What are you wanting to say when you become the speaker? Do you have new insights or has your point of view changed?

Brené Brown captures the spirit of contemplative silence in what she refers to as *stillness*. "It's about creating a clearing. It's opening up an emotionally clutter-free space and allowing ourselves to feel and think and dream and question." (Brown 2010, 108) We can experience this stillness after one person speaks and before the next begins. Brown's notion of stillness includes the necessity of bringing an openness to the quiet so that we can take the speaker's words to heart and not mindlessly drift back to our own comfortable, prepared position. Think of the Gesture as opening your heart while listening, and contemplative silence as helping to keep it open just a bit longer.

> **Think of the Gesture as opening your heart while listening, and contemplative silence as helping to keep it open just a bit longer.**

Equally important in the silence is that we let the speaker know that what they said truly matters. We do not jump in immediately to speak, thereby negating what we just heard. We show respect and demonstrate that we are truly considering what we heard during the contemplative silence.

You begin the contemplative silence by taking a breath. Then take another breath. If the silence seems to be mutually understood, you can just keep breathing and thinking and considering. Or you could say, "I have a lot to say, but I'd like to take a few minutes to think." You can sit there, take a few notes, or go take a short walk. You could say, "I'm going to get a bit of fresh air; how about we meet back here in ten minutes?"

> We need to be more courageous in embracing the suffering aspect of the transformative process. Happiness is not found in evading the rough patches of the journey, and cannot be identified with little surges of happy hormones. That is not happiness, it is addiction!
>
> —Schlitz, Vieten, Amorok, *Living Deeply*

Contemplative silence allows the words to sink in for both speaker and listener, and also allows time to reflect. This quiet time before listener turns into speaker is vital to the success of the Gesture.

Conflict Transformation

The *Tell Me More Gesture* is an effective method of communication during conflict because it assumes that, when in conflict, we are concerned with not only the issues, but also how we are treated. We are able to gain skills at maintaining or reestablishing connection when we disagree and when someone is acting out at us. In their theory of transformative mediation, Bush and Folger (2005) refer to the ability to move from seeing ourselves strictly as individuals to seeing ourselves as connected as conflict transformation.

> Obtaining satisfying and fair outcomes is undoubtedly important to parties in conflict, as is minimizing the economic and emotional cost of doing so. However, the importance of these benefits rests on the assumption that people are separate beings who are affected by but not essentially connected to each other, so that meeting needs can be accomplished without necessarily changing the quality of the interaction itself. By contrast, the importance of conflict transformation rests on the assumption that people are, by their essential nature, both separate and connected beings, who are distressed whenever negative interaction between them continues, even if their separate needs get satisfied (Bush and Folger 2005, page 35).

Notice in the Betty and Brad story (page 48) that in the end, the Gesture satisfied Betty in both her need for being an individual, that is, she felt personal success and self-respect for accomplishing the Gesture, and her need to feel connected to others, in this case, her husband. There is balance in the Gesture. It serves the listener as both an individual and a person needing to be connected to others.

Moving Forward

In chapter 3 you have learned that, to succeed at the Gesture, you must give recognition (the feeling of getting listened to) until the speaker is all-the-way done. You understand that giving recognition is not a selfless act. It is has great benefits to you, the listener, and understanding these motivations will be key to staying on track with the Gesture. During times of conflict, the Gesture is, most importantly, a gift to yourself. You also learned the third component to the Gesture: the need for contemplative silence after the speaker is finished. Before moving on, spend ten to fifteen minutes completing the following journal entries.

> There is a difference between truly listening and waiting for your turn to talk.
>
> —Ralph Waldo Emerson, American Poet

Journal Entry 3.1

Based on your experience during Exercise 3.1 (page 50), make some notes about the things you perceived in the speaker, as well as in yourself. Here are the prompts from the exercise: *Do they seem buoyed by your extra interest? Do they talk more in depth as well as longer? Do their speech patterns change? Does their mood lighten or get more intense? Do you find out more than you would have if you had done your normal style and amount of listening? Did you feel more interested as the time went by?*

_____

_____

_____

_____

_____

_____

_____

_____

_____

_____

_____

_____

_____

_____

_____

_____

_____

Journal Entry 3.2

Do you have any worries about using the Gesture? Are there particular people in your life for whom you think this will work well or not so well?

_____

_____

_____

_____

_____

_____

_____

_____

_____

_____

_____

_____

_____

_____

_____

_____

_____

Chapter 4:
THE ART OF
REFLECTION—PART 1

In chapter 2, you learned the *safety net phrases*; now it is time to make the *Tell Me More Gesture* your own. It is important to understand that listening during times of conflict must be deep and it must be interactive. Deep listening means that you look for the depth in what the speaker is saying, regardless of how it is being presented to you. Interactive listening means that you are giving verbal and visual clues to the speaker that you are deeply considering their statements.

> **Listening during times of conflict must be deep, and it must be interactive.**

The essence of the Gesture is to accept someone exactly as they are, to let them know that it is safe to be their imperfect self with you, and to allow them, when they are upset, to behave in ways that you may not like, but that you understand. The speaker is being rude, perhaps cruel, and you don't enjoy this, but you know that the "bad" behavior is a symptom of their feeling disempowered. You understand that shouting and name-calling are not signs of strength—they are signs of weakness. This is how people behave when they are in conflict.

What Is a Reflection?

In dialogue, a reflection is a statement that literally reflects or shows back to the speaker what the speaker is saying. Ideally, a reflection not only repeats or restates what was said, but also captures the nuance and the energy of the statement. That is, we must consider not only the words, but also the intonation, the facial expressions, the gesturing, and the overall expression of the speaker. Reflecting is a vital part of any productive communication because it serves as a mirror for the speaker. They are speaking for a reason: to feel and to be understood.

> Listening is not merely not talking, though even that is beyond most of our powers; it means taking a vigorous, human interest in what is being told us. You can listen like a blank wall or like a splendid auditorium where every sound comes back fuller and richer.
>
> —Alice Duer Miller, American writer

Making reflections that are consistent with the Gesture means that you welcome the emotions and behaviors of the speaker by making statements that help them feel deep-down listened to. In doing this, you help the speaker, and you help yourself as the listener, get clearer and feel calmer and stronger. Your presence as a wholehearted reflector is exactly the thing that is most likely to help the speaker calm down, although your intention is to help them do whatever they need to do—they may need to get more upset!

There are two main types of reflections in the *Tell Me More Gesture*:

1. Quick phrase reflections
2. Short list reflections (chapter 5)

Quick Phrase Reflections

Use quick phrases when the speaker is the most upset. They may be loud and using threatening speech. This is a temporary state. The key is to lean in when the speaker is out of their mind with anger and distress. Your first impulse is likely to recoil, but you can recover quickly and move to the Gesture, knowing it is the most expedient and productive way to get through the conflict. During these times of high conflict, making *quick phrase reflections* might look something like this:

> Go and love someone exactly as they are. And then watch how quickly they transform into the greatest, truest version of themselves. When one feels seen and appreciated in their own essence, one is instantly empowered.
>
> —Wes Angelozzi,
> American writer

SPEAKER: "You're a royal bitch! You must be having your period. I think—"

LISTENER: [leaning forward] "I'm a bitch!"

SPEAKER: "Yes, you are, you've been a mean grump for three days."

LISTENER: [leaning forward] "Three days!"

SPEAKER: "It's been grueling. I can't take it anymore."

LISTENER: "It seems hopeless, it sounds like."

SPEAKER: "Yes, I can't take it! Three days of your moodiness and griping!"

LISTENER: "Three days of it!"

SPEAKER: "Well, it might be two, I'm not sure. But it's been awful."

LISTENER: "It's *really* bad."

[And so on.]

Let's look at what makes this a successful interaction. The following ten skills are being utilized in this short exchange.

The Ten Fundamentals of Effective Reflections

1. Be brief.
2. Choose topic or emotion.
3. Reflect often.
4. Match the vocabulary.
5. Match the energy.

6. Go to the heat.
7. Open up the conversation.
8. Exude empathy.
9. Reduce the use of qualifiers.
10. Interject.

These skills are the essentials to becoming proficient at the Gesture, so let's examine each of them in depth. They will also be utilized in *short list reflections* (chapter 5).

1. Be brief. Your statements as the listener should be extremely short. When someone is really upset, they might be ranting, shouting, and not giving much specific information. You need to reflect the essence of what the speaker is saying, letting go of any details. A brief reflection invites more dialogue, which is the goal.

> Brevity in reflections invites more dialogue.

Often listeners, in their quest to be the best listener, repeat back a detailed account of everything the speaker said. The listener goes on and on, sometimes taking more time than the speaker originally used, in order to prove that every detail was absorbed. Know this: A lengthy reflection is generally more about the listener than it is about the speaker. It is your job to give concise reflections so that the speaker can continue. You are not taking over the conversation. You are paving the way for the speaker to say more.

Example 1: Be brief

Inflammatory statement: "You are the most selfish person in
the whole world!"

Not-so-good reflection: "So you're saying that I'm really
selfish and that there isn't anyone as selfish as I am
anywhere else in the world."

Good reflection: "I'm completely selfish!"

Coaching note: You can see in the above example that the not-so-great reflection is actually longer than the speaker's statement. This is definitely stealing the limelight and will not encourage the speaker to tell you more. The good reflection allows the speaker to know that you understand, and it is brief so that the speaker feels welcome to continue on. By the way, the more you say, the more likely you are to prove their point about being selfish or self-absorbed. Check out the following story:

■   ■   ■

Matthew and Larry had been together for over fifteen years. They were recently married, and both felt upset that they were fighting increasingly more often since then, and, in fact, had been discussing separating permanently. They came in looking for help not only with the conflict, but also to learn about ways to communicate better. We spent an hour or more learning about the Gesture, and they both appeared devoted to giving it a good try. Larry was the more introverted of the two, and Matthew admitted that he tended to interrupt Larry. But Matthew was being careful to not interrupt in the session. At one point Larry said, "I'm tired of all the fighting. It wears me out and makes me feel hopeless." Matthew began his reflection by saying, "You're feeling hopeless. And you're exhausted." Perfect. But then Matthew continued on: "I totally understand what you're saying! I'm so tired of it all. It makes me wonder how we managed through these seventeen years together." Matthew paused as if he had more to say and then looked straight at Larry. Then he looked to me and I gave him a little smile. We all just sat there. Matthew placed his forehead on the table and started to howl with laughter. Then Larry joined in and I did my best to not break out laughing, too. Matthew looked up with tears from laughing and embarrassment, and practically shouted at Larry, "Tell me more!" More laughter ensued.

■   ■   ■

Matthew's verbose reflection was a result of his enthusiasm. This is common, but it is still not an excuse to go on and on.

2. Choose the topic or the emotion. In a heated moment, coming up with a good reflection can feel daunting. You can simplify the task by mirroring back the essence of what they said by choosing the information they are giving you or the emotion they are displaying or describing. This is up to you, your intuition, and your own comfort in naming difficult things. You choose the words or the sentiment, or both. At any time if you are at a loss for what to say, you can go back to the *safety net phrases* (page 28).

> To say that a person feels listened to means a lot more than just their ideas get heard. It's a sign of respect. It makes people feel valued.
>
> —Deborah Tannen,
> Professor of Linguistics

Example 2: Choose the topic or the emotion

Inflammatory statement: "You are the most self-absorbed person in the whole world. I can't take it anymore!"

Good reflection using the topic: "I'm self-absorbed!"

Good reflection using the emotion: "Wow, you've had it!"

(This is a *safety net phrase* but also describes their emotion.)

Coaching note: Notice that the reflection here does not name the emotion too specifically. We are not trying to label or pin the speaker down by saying something like, "You're feeling deranged with anger!" We are trying to demonstrate that we are interested and that we care, so that they can continue on. If the speaker tells you that they are angry, or if they demonstrate it to you, then "You're angry!" or "You're furious!" might be fine. Know that if you miss the mark, they will tell you, and this is part of good communication. They might say, "I'm not angry, I'm sad!" Your missing the mark on your reflection still helps them get clearer.

3. Reflect often. Reflecting often accomplishes two things. First, it keeps you engaged as the listener. Second, it sends a message to the speaker that you are supportive, no matter what the topic, no matter what the emotion, and no matter how long they continue to speak. Note: Once the speaker calms down and starts talking in full sentences that contain real information about their distress, then you can stop reflecting often and start using short list reflections (chapter 5).

Example 3: Reflect often

SPEAKER: "You are the most self-absorbed person in the whole world! I can't take it anymore!"

LISTENER: "I'm self-absorbed."

SPEAKER: "Yes, you are! You only think of yourself."

LISTENER: "I'm really selfish!"

SPEAKER: "I've just had it! I can't take it anymore."

LISTENER: "Wow, tell me more!"

SPEAKER: "Well, I will! You've used me up. You've taken advantage of my good nature and now I'm done. I'm not going to take it anymore. You are a complete narcissist."

LISTENER: "You've really had it!"

SPEAKER: "Yes, I have. You don't consult me about what I want. You just go ahead and make plans and don't consider my time or my schedule. You do this all the time!"

Coaching note: Here you can see that the listener makes *quick phrase reflections* for the first three exchanges and then, during the fourth exchange, instead of making a reflection, the listener pauses and lets the speaker continue on. Notice that in the speaker's last statement, there is specific information that the listener has not previously heard. The speaker is beginning to talk with more clarity.

Know that you can overdo this, so you must use "reflect often" with a measure of care. After a few quick statements back and forth between speaker and listener, you may very well want to pause for a moment. You need to be aware of the speaker's needs and comfort level. The point is to invite more discussion, so lean forward and reflect often, as long as seems tolerable to the speaker.

> Sell your cleverness and buy bewilderment.
>
> —Rumi,
> 13th-century Sufi Mystic

4. Match the vocabulary. (Don't try to sound smart.) It is important that you use a style of language that is comfortable to the speaker. You are trying to encourage the speaker to say more, not to impress them with how smart you are.

Example 4: Match the vocabulary

Inflammatory statement: "You are the most self-absorbed person in the whole world! I can't take it anymore!"

Not-so-good reflection: "I'm a narcissist!" or "You're completely depleted!"

Good reflection: "I'm really selfish!" or "You've had it!"

Coaching note: These not-so-good reflections seem to be more about the listener proving their vocabulary and intelligence than about making the speaker feel listened to. This can feel patronizing. Simple reflections are almost always better—and quicker, too.

■　■　■

A few years back I was helping with training mediation students at a law school. These students were very intelligent and amazingly adept at learning the new skills of mediation, very different from other skills they had been learning as law students. They had learned about neutrality and the importance of party choice, and they seemed eager to try on the mediator role, which necessarily meant giving up their advocate role. These students excelled at remaining neutral and allowing for party self-determination, but they struggled to let go of using overly sophisticated vocabulary while practicing reflections during role plays. For example, in a scenario about two adult siblings, one of the role players exclaimed, "We never talk anymore. You don't talk to me! And you're so controlling with Mom's money." Jordan, the mediator in the role play, then reflected formally, "It seems you're concerned about communication and monetary issues."

■ ■ ■

You can see that Jordan's reflection has a different tone from what the role player exhibited; it sounds lofty. This can feel disempowering and discouraging for the participant. Jordan doesn't sound curious for more information. It appears he has it neatly wrapped up and probably doesn't need to know any more. A better reflection would simply be, "He doesn't talk to you anymore and he's being controlling." The simplicity of the statement is clear and comforting to hear back, and it inherently invites the speaker to say more. Likewise with the Gesture, using vocabulary that sounds superior, especially at a time when someone is very upset, may serve to shut someone down instead of open them up. In the art of reflecting, it is better to be compassionate than smart.

> In the art of reflecting, it is better to be compassionate than smart.

5. Match the energy. It is important to not only to match the speaker's vocabulary style, but also their energy or emotion. When someone is extremely upset and swearing, for example, you don't have to yell and swear, but it helps if you echo some of their animated energy in your reflections. You can do this by sitting attentively, leaning forward, and letting the tone of your voice be lively and earnest. There is a huge temptation to try to be completely calm as the reflector, but this can feel detached or judgmental to the speaker. Try matching the energy and see how it feels for you. It may take some getting used to.

> Being heard is so close to being loved that for the average person, they are almost indistinguishable.
>
> —David Augsburger, American Anabaptist author

Example 5: Match the energy

Inflammatory statement: "You are the most self-absorbed person in the whole world! I can't take it anymore!"

Not-so-good reflection: The listener sits attentively and erectly listening to the speaker. The listener's hands are in her lap. She is a little wary so she decides to play an observer stance and not get too involved. She states, "I'm really selfish."

Good reflection: The listener sits attentively, leaning forward slightly with her elbows on her knees. She is a little wary but she decides to remain forward and make sure the speaker feels encouraged to say more. She says, "I'm really selfish!"

Coaching note: In the not-so-good reflection, the listener's words are adequate, but the listener's posture is rigid. This is not a crime, of course, and is far better than many other reflections. Certainly the speaker is likely to respond, but one of our goals is for the speaker to talk and behave as freely as possible. Stiffness in the listener can be perceived as judgment by the speaker; leaning forward is a way to help avoid this miscommunication. Being met with the warmer and more animated gesture of the good reflection will elicit a freer response.

As an example of reflecting the energy, think back to the story about Grace and her behavior in the boardroom. Here is the rest of the story :

■ ■ ■

The board members' reactions to Grace's eruption were to be silent. We waited, trying not to stare, and her ranting and swearing continued. After what seemed like forever, but which was likely a few minutes, I reached over to Grace, who was sitting next to me, gently touched her leg, and quietly, with a calming voice, said to her, "Grace. Shhh. You're misbehaving." I meant this sweetly. I meant this to be help for her. I knew she would feel bad later about her behavior. Grace proceeded to turn her wrath on me, spewing hateful remarks. The episode ended with Grace storming out of the room. The members turned to me to comfort me and I kept telling them, "No, no, this is not about me." I felt so sad about Grace. Grace never returned to the board.

■ ■ ■

My response to Grace was intended to be empathic, but to Grace it must have felt incredibly judgmental. I had used the word "misbehaving," which is full of innuendo. It's the first word that came to my mind, and at the moment, it felt like an emergency. So I used the word, thinking my intentions would be clear. And I had talked so quietly it probably made her voice seem even louder. The hidden message there is: *See. This is normal behavior. Remember? You should be talking quietly.* The truth is, I was trying to get her to stop her behavior. I was not listening to her words nor her emotions. If I had it to do over again, I hope that I would react much differently. I hope that I would stand up or at least sit up tall and tell her, "Oh, Grace! You've really had it!" Perhaps then she would have felt invited to say more about how she felt, perhaps then she would have been able to calm down on her own accord, perhaps then she wouldn't have felt judged—and perhaps then she wouldn't have had to leave the room, and ultimately the board, in anger and embarrassment.

6. Go to the heat. In any given moment during the Gesture you have many choices about what to say to make the speaker feel heard. When in doubt, go to the heat by reflecting the most uncomfortable statement that you heard. We make a lot of assumptions about a person's capacity when we avoid talking about the tough stuff.

> We make a lot of assumptions about a person's capacity when we avoid talking about the tough stuff.

Going to the heat takes some courage, but it is a tremendously connecting gesture because it tells the speaker that you are accepting them as they are, even when they are upset with you. You are, in effect, putting your head in the lion's mouth. When you go

> Sometimes fear won't go away, so you'll have to do it afraid.
>
> —Unknown

to the heat, you let the speaker know that you are accepting them exactly as they are in that moment.

Example 6: Go to the heat

Inflammatory statement: "You are the most self-absorbed person in the whole world! I can't take it anymore!"
Not-so-good reflection: "I'm sort of selfish."
Good reflection: "I'm completely selfish!"

> It's a rare person who wants to hear what he doesn't want to hear.
>
> —Dick Cavett, American television personality

Coaching note: Notice that the not-so-good reflection indeed names what the speaker is saying, i.e., "selfish," but diminishes the impact by saying "sort of." This is not a crime, and the reflection may do no harm. However, the better reflection in the above example would be, "I'm completely selfish!" because it is much closer to getting at the upsetness that the speaker is demonstrating. The speaker then has the opportunity to say more, such as, "Yes! You really hurt my feelings when you didn't consider my opinion about the new car." Now, there is specific information from the speaker, which is clearer and more conversational.

Going to the heat promotes a deep and forgiving relationship. It is true that people say things out of anger. It happens often. But if we find empathy for them and leave an opening for them to continue, we find they are acting angrily because they have been harmed or shut down in the past. There is information in the upsetness. We are not encouraging people to be brutal to one another, we are

> **There is information in the upsetness.**

encouraging them to be free to be who they are so that they have the opportunity get unstuck and move forward. Tamping down a situation merely makes things worse, and then the conflict may intensify or come out sideways later.

> Courage is what it takes to stand up and speak; courage is also what it takes to sit down and listen.
>
> —Winston Churchill,
> British Prime Minister

Personally and professionally, I do tend to put my head in the lion's mouth. This does not feel like a choice to me. It feels like a gravitational pull to get to the heart of the matter. When someone is truthful with me, it honors me, even if it is difficult to hear. As a mediator, when someone is vulnerable enough to be upset around me, I want it to be apparent that I am not judging them. I know what it feels like to be upset, I know what it feels like to not get heard, and

When someone is truthful with you, it honors you, even if it is difficult to hear.

I know what it feels like to feel free and accepted. Going to the heat, by naming the thing they are most upset about, is a gesture that is normalizing and accepting.

7. Open up the conversation. Making reflections that help the conversation remain as open as possible is an important key to success in listening to someone who is upset. It's also a skill worth developing for regular conversations. Your reflections should help the speaker take the conversation in any direction they choose. We are letting go of fact-finding. We therefore stop asking for more information as if we need proof, such as, "How long did that last?" or "How do you know that?" and we start saying things like, "Oh my goodness, tell me more!" or "Holy smokes, this has been terrible for you!"

Example 7: Open up the conversation

Inflammatory statement: "You are the most self-absorbed person in the whole world! I can't take it anymore!"
Not-so-good reflection: "What do you mean by self-absorbed?"
Good reflection: "I'm completely self-absorbed!" and/or "Tell me more!"

Coaching note: In this example, the not-so-good reflection steers the speaker to respond about one particular aspect of their statement. It can sound like the listener is quizzing or requiring proof. This is a defensive move and not in line with the Gesture's goal of opening up the conversation. After hearing the good reflection, the speaker might continue on to a different topic by saying something like, "And you're also a bully!" Alternatively, the speaker might take a different turn and say, "Well, I appreciate that yesterday you considered me when you were making plans, but I still feel you are so selfish." We will never know what the speaker might have said if we hadn't steered the conversation.

> You cannot truly listen to anyone and do anything else at the same time.
>
> —M. Scott Peck,
> American psychiatrist

8. Exude empathy. Finding empathy and demonstrating it to the speaker is an important attribute of your reflections. Can you feel empathy for someone who is yelling at or accusing you? Yes, you can. You don't have to agree with someone to find empathy for them. You can understand the panic they are feeling. You have behaved in ways, in the past, that you are not proud of, so you can find empathy for someone who is also not behaving their best. Empathy is discussed at length in chapter 7, but for now, know that when you give an empathic response to someone who is upset, regardless of the words you use, it is the single most productive thing you can do because it restores the human connection between speaker and listener.

Example 8: Exude empathy

Inflammatory statement: "You are the most self-absorbed person in the whole world! I can't take it anymore!"

Not-so-good reflection: [sitting straight] "I'm self-absorbed?"

Good reflection: [leaning forward] "I'm completely self-absorbed!" and/or "Tell me more!"

Coaching note: The manner in which the reflection is delivered is crucial in demonstrating empathy. In the not-so-good reflection, the listener asks the question as if it is pretty hard to believe that they might be self-absorbed. The good reflection is good because the listener is leaning forward and truly believing that the speaker is serious in their assertion. Regardless of the words, the listener's crucial gesture is their demonstrating that they care to know more and have empathy for the person who is so upset.

> I care about who you are, who you have been, who you want to be. I open myself to you to listen and learn about you. I cherish you, not just my fantasy of who you are, not just who I need you to be, but who you really are.
>
> —Betty Berzon,
> American psychotherapist

9. Reduce the use of qualifiers. Qualifying phrases are the little comments the listener makes, often with good intentions, that give the speaker hints about the listener's thoughts and feelings. Qualifiers sound like this:

"<u>So what you're saying is that</u> I only think of myself."
"<u>From your point of view</u> we are spending too much money."
"<u>You believe that</u> I don't help enough."

The message when using qualifiers is that you don't necessarily agree but that you are listening. This gives you, the listener, some solace, but it is a way of manipulating the conversation to be about you, the listener, instead of the speaker. Qualifiers do not help open up a conversation. They keep a boundary between speaker and listener, which can inhibit the speaker from telling you more.

Example 9: Reduce the use of qualifiers

Inflammatory statement: "You are the most self-absorbed
      person in the whole world! I can't take it anymore!"
Not-so-good reflection: "So you're saying that I'm selfish."
Good reflection: "I'm selfish."

Coaching note: Let's be real, we all use qualifying phrases in our everyday speech, so the idea here is to be aware of the message they send and to greatly reduce them. When you are first learning the *Tell Me More Gesture*, it can be uncomfortable to try this because you feel that you may be misunderstood and that the speaker will think that you are in agreement. This is not the case, especially if you lean forward and look like you care about what the speaker is saying. Try it and see what you think. By the way, reducing the use of qualifiers also serves to shorten our reflections—all the better!

10. Interject. Although it may feel counterintuitive, when the speaker is especially emotional and vociferous, it is important to interject reflections and make them often. You are, in a way, interrupting, to let them know that you are right there with them. Generally, this sort of interruption feels good to the speaker. They feel supported and invited to say more.

> Listening looks easy, but it's not simple. Every head is a world.
>
> —Cuban Proverb

You will be amazed how a short, accurate reflection of what the speaker is thinking or feeling encourages them to say more without your actually saying, "Tell me more." The speaker will gladly continue. It is key here that your intention is to support them and not to shut them up by your interjecting. Attempting to stop someone from speaking is not part of the Gesture.

Example 10: Interject

Inflammatory speaker statement: "You are the most self-absorbed person in the whole world! I can't take it anymore!"

Good reflection: "I'm self-absorbed."

Speaker: "Yes, you are. I'm at my wit's end about the way you treat me."

Good reflection: "Oh my, you've had it!"

Speaker: "Yes, I have. I give and give and you just take advantage of me."

Good reflection: "I'm taking advantage."

Speaker: "You are!" [crying] "And I feel so unappreciated for all I do."

Good reflection: "Oh my, I don't appreciate you."

Speaker: "You don't, you don't. You rarely say thank you. You just sit there and eat dinner and barely even talk to me."

Good reflection:" I don't say thank you."

Speaker: "And you don't talk to me!"

Good reflection: "And we don't talk."

Speaker: "Yes, yes." [tearing up] "I really miss that."

Good reflection: "That's so sad." [pause] "Is there more?"

[And so on.]

> Who speaks, sows;
> Who listens, reaps.
>
> —Argentine proverb

Coaching note: You can see that the listener interjects by making a reflection after each statement. You can sense that a rhythm develops. Remember that this is an exchange that is occurring while the speaker is extremely upset. In a regular conversation, we likely do not interject in this way, but in these highly emotional situations it is surprisingly helpful.

Notice that the speaker started by talking about the listener being self-absorbed, and by the end, the topic had changed to the fact that the speaker misses talking with the listener. If, instead of reflecting, the listener had asked a question such as, "How can you say that? When have I been self-absorbed?" in order to make the speaker prove their statement, the speaker may never have felt safe enough to be vulnerable and verbalize their feelings.

Please also note that the listener does not rush in to fix the situation by defending or by making a quick apology. Although these are great temptations, the empathic tone of voice and quick reflections provide the speaker with the most options and with a true invitation to talk freely. There will be plenty of time for defenses or apologies, if necessary, after the speaker is finished.

These *ten fundamentals of effective reflections* are the ABCs of how to help someone feel listened to when they are upset. They are meant to free you up, not hamstring you. It takes practice to apply them in the moment, not only because there may be new ideas for you, but also because it is hard to accomplish this when you also may be upset. Chapter 8, "Get Hold of Yourself," will help you sort out the topic of your upsetness.

Now for some practice. The overall idea for *quick phrase reflections* is to *just name it*. You must have the courage to name the thing that is being said that is likely very hot, whether because of the topic or because of the emotion, or both. You must have the courage to name it, and to do so in the most open way possible. Please do this exercise before moving on.

> I only wish I could find an institute that teaches people how to listen. Business people need to listen at least as much as they need to talk.
>
> —Lee Iacocca,
> Former CEO Chrysler Corporation

Exercise 4.1   Just Name It

[Duration: ten minutes]

For each upset statement, write down a good, quick phrase reflection using either the topic or the emotion. After you write it down, say it aloud. This is really good practice. Notice the first few statements are more general upset statements and the latter ones are personal in nature. The first two are completed for you, as examples.

1. SPEAKER: "I can't get this! This is too hard!"
    LISTENER: It's too hard! [topic] or You've had it! [emotion]

2. SPEAKER: "That's it! I quit!" [regarding employment]
    LISTENER: You're done! [topic] or You've had it! [emotion]

3. SPEAKER: "If it rains one more day I'm going to kill somebody!"
    LISTENER: _____

4. SPEAKER: "I'm not going!"
    LISTENER: _____

5. SPEAKER: "Everyone hates me!"
    LISTENER: _____

6. SPEAKER: "You're wearing *that* out tonight?!"
    LISTENER: _____

7. SPEAKER: "You are completely clueless!"
    LISTENER: _____

8. SPEAKER: "You only think of yourself!"
    LISTENER: _____

9. SPEAKER: "I hate you!"
    LISTENER: _____

Exercise 4.1   Just Name It

Let's Try It Together

1.   SPEAKER: "I can't get this! This is too hard!"

There is temptation for the listener to say something encouraging here, such as, "Of course you can do it. Maybe a break would help." Believe it or not, this is a type of fixing or problem-solving. If instead we say, <u>"It's too hard!"</u> [topic] or <u>"You've had it!"</u> [emotion], the speaker then has the opportunity to say more about their frustration instead of being shut down by a suggested solution.

2.   SPEAKER: "That's it! I quit!" [regarding employment]

You may be tempted to say, "Why?" And then you might want to add, "You can't afford to just quit!" Asking why fulfills our own need for more information as the listener. Then telling the speaker they can't afford to quit is, first of all, something they have already realized and second, will feel judgmental. Making a quick reflection such as, <u>"Wow, you're really done!"</u> [topic] or <u>"You've really had it!"</u> [emotion] will allow the speaker to say more. They may tell you why, they may say how sorry they are that they've quit, or they may tell you how empowered they feel. It's up to them.

3.   SPEAKER: "If it rains one more day I'm going to kill somebody!"

This is an opportunity for some people to go into fix-it mode and say, "Have you ever tried a sunlight lamp? I love mine!" or "It's not that bad." But if you say, <u>"Boy, the weather is really getting you down!"</u> [topic] or <u>"It's been horrible!"</u> [emotion], then you are leaving room for the speaker to tell you more.

4.   SPEAKER: "I'm not going!"

Again, we want to go into fix-it mode by saying, "You'll have fun!" Or we pepper them with questions: "Why not? Are you nervous?" But if you simply say, <u>"You've decided not to go!"</u> [topic] or <u>"Wow, tell me more!"</u> [emotion], then you are likely to hear more about what is important to them.

5. SPEAKER: "Everyone hates me!"

    We are definitely tempted to refute the statement, such as "Oh honey! That's not true! You have lots of friends!" This is a fix-it move that attempts to use logic at a time when someone is quite emotional, and it doesn't invite more discussion. You could simply say, "Oh my, everyone hates you," [topic] or you could try "Wow, what's going on?" [emotion] or "Wow, tell me more!" [safety net phrase] Both help the speaker to say more without any attempt to steer their response. "What's going on?" leaves an opening for them to say more about specifically what happened or how they are doing in general.

6. SPEAKER: "You're wearing that out tonight!?"

    Responding with sarcasm is common when we're feeling personally attacked. In the moment, it might feel good to say, "Like you're one to judge! Who made you the fashion police?" (lashing out). This feels personal, but you can think to yourself, We have different opinions. Then you can say, "Oh! You don't like what I'm wearing— tell me more," [topic] or "Wow, you're upset! Tell me more." [emotion]

7. SPEAKER: "You are completely clueless!"

    This is a statement that can really hurt. However, it is evident that the speaker is at their wit's end. If the statement catches you off guard you can rely on a safety net phrase like "Wow, you've had it," or "Tell me more." If you can manage it, you can say, "I don't have a clue!" or "I'm an idiot," [topic] or "Wow, you're upset!" [emotion] Any of these statements will encourage the speaker to say more.

8. SPEAKER: "You only think of yourself!"

    "Tell me more" [safety net phrase] is an effective response to any of these strong statements (7-9). You could also simply say, "I'm really selfish!" [topic]

9. SPEAKER: "I hate your guts!"

    "Wow, you've had it!" [safety net phrase, emotion] might work well for this statement. Or you could say, "You really hate me! Tell me more." [topic]

Moving Forward

In chapter 4, you learned the importance of making reflections to help the speaker feel listened to. You learned specific skills in the *ten fundamentals of effective reflections* to be used in making *quick phrase reflections* (as well as to be used in *short list reflections* in chapter 5). Remember that *quick phrase reflections* are to be used in the heat of the moment, when the speaker is really upset. Before moving on to the next chapter, please take ten to fifteen minutes to consider and complete the following journal entries. Here is a review list of the *ten fundamentals of effective reflections* for use in the following journal entries:

1. Be brief.
2. Choose topic or emotion.
3. Reflect often.
4. Match the vocabulary.
5. Match the energy.

6. Go to the heat.
7. Open up the conversation.
8. Exude empathy.
9. Reduce the use of qualifiers.
10. Interject.

> It's taken years, but part of my own personal growth has involved deciding that I can learn something from even the most annoying person.
>
> —Auliq Ice,
> American rapper

Journal Entry 4.1

Some of the *ten fundamentals of effective reflections* may intuitively resonate with you more than others. Use the space below to list three or four that ring truest for you. Why do you think this is the case?

_____

_____

_____

_____

_____

_____

_____

_____

_____

_____

_____

Note: The fundamentals that you listed here are personal strengths that you bring to the Gesture. These come most easily to you, and you will be able to rely on these skills as you begin practicing. These are attributes that you may already, naturally, demonstrate when listening in regular circumstances, and they are assets that you can begin to utilize during a conflict.

Journal Entry 4.2

Consider which of the *ten fundamentals of effective reflections* feel difficult for you to integrate into your everyday life. List three or four below and explain why they might be more challenging.

_____

_____

_____

_____

_____

_____

_____

_____

_____

_____

_____

_____

_____

_____

_____

Note: Whatever your challenges are, look for conversations in your daily life, when you are *not* in conflict, to practice getting more comfortable with them. For example, when you are listening to a friend complain about a bad experience with her boyfriend or a coworker, you can practice going to the heat by saying, "Wow, he cheated on you!" or "You're really upset!" or "Tell me more," instead of "What a jerk! What did he do to you?"

Please join the Readers' Forum at Janet's website: tellmemoregesture.com. This is a private forum where readers can discuss their successes and struggles of working on the Tell Me More Gesture.

Chapter 5:
THE ART OF
REFLECTION—PART 2

Short List Reflections

At some point in a conflict or difficult discussion, you will notice that you start hearing more information and less name-calling or other explosive language. The speaker is giving more details, although it still may sound blaming or unpleasant. This is a good time to stop *quick phrase reflections* and begin waiting until the end of their thought, probably the equivalent of a paragraph or two if they are very upset, and do a *short list reflection*.

> Listening is the key. The whole objective of a howl is to be heard.
>
> —Amit Pandey, *The Retro Man*

In this style of reflection, you are supplying a summary of what you have heard very recently, organized in a short list, usually in two to four points. Notice in the following example that the listener does not say, nor give a hint about, whether they agree or disagree.

SPEAKER: "You've been really difficult lately. A royal pain in the butt. I'm having trouble getting my work done because you seem to feel free to interrupt me at any moment with your incessant complaining. I'm on deadline and you don't care!"

LISTENER: "Hang on. Let me just make sure I get this. You're on a deadline and I don't care. I'm a royal pain in the butt. My bitching and moaning is getting in the way of your work. Is there more?"

SPEAKER: "Yes! And I'm the one who's busy and all you do is sit around and do your little projects and then I end up having to do the dishes even though I just don't have time! I can't do everything!"

LISTENER: "So in addition to my complaining and interrupting, you are having to do the dishes when you're already swamped. And I'm just sitting around and you're doing everything."

[And so on.]

> None of us is perfect. All of us make mistakes. And close relationships are a place where we're bound to make them. In fact, until we've seen someone's darkness we don't really know them.
>
> —Marianne Williamson, American spiritual teacher

Coaching note: Even though the speaker's statements got more heated, this is a success because our goal is to open up the conversation, not to control it or tamp it down.

Short list reflections help in several ways: the speaker will know that you understand, will get more clear on what is bothering them, and, if you deliver the statements empathically, will know that you care. Utilizing the *ten fundamentals of effective reflections*, your reflections will have the same attributes as the *quick phrase reflections*, but will sound very different because they are organized in a list.

■ ■ ■

As a mother and her teenage daughter (who had been kicked out of the family home) entered the mediation room, there was a chill in the air, but interestingly, they sat down next to each other. So my co-mediator and I sat across from them both. Donna, the mom, was really upset with her daughter, Claire. Donna felt Claire's behavior was well beyond house rules, and Donna made no bones about her feelings. She looked directly at me and told us a litany of issues she had with her daughter. And then added, "And she's a slut." I found empathy for the mother's struggle and began reflecting things back that I had heard. I leaned forward and said, "So Claire doesn't obey your rules. And she doesn't help take care of her siblings." As I made this short list of the things I had heard, I glanced at Claire to see how she was doing. She seemed to be patiently waiting her turn. I looked back at Donna and continued, "She stays out until well after curfew if she comes home at all." I leaned in toward her even further, tilted my head a bit, and without pause I said, "And I heard you say Claire is a slut." Soon after my reflection, Donna softened her tone and said, "I really don't know what she does since I kicked her out, but she really is a good girl at heart." And later, after she heard Claire talk, including her wishes to work on her art, Donna noted to us, "She is a lovely artist!"

In our debrief after the session, my co-mediator, Beth, and I discussed my decision to reflect back the inflammatory statement(s). Beth was amazed by the positive effect of reflecting back what Donna had said, even in front of Claire. Beth noted, "Well, of course, the daughter had already heard these things. It's not like it's a surprise to her!" And we noticed together that it was apparent to both Donna and Claire that I was not taking sides.

■ ■ ■

This is a good example of a *short list reflection* and of going to the heat. I reflected back the extremely inflammatory statements of Donna without Claire assuming that I was taking sides. This is an important lesson. When first learning the Gesture, people often tell me that they are concerned if they reflect back what they hear from the speaker, the speaker will then assume that they are in agreement. Know that your giving empathic reflections will rarely, if ever, appear to the speaker that you are in agreement. To the contrary, they are trust building because the speaker feels welcomed to be their true, upset self without being judged.

> And he listened to me. That was the thing he did, as if he was trying to fill himself up with all the sound he could hear.
>
> —Ray Bradbury,
> *The Illustrated Man*

Short list reflections are effective, not only because they show understanding and caring, but also because they restrain the listener from making long, rambling reflections. This expounding takes the focus away from the speaker and is more about the listener showing what they know. Concise, simple reflections are always better.

Know that *short list reflections* prove that you have been listening and demonstrate your interest, not only because of your words, but also because of the energy and warmth of your delivery. You organize a list in your mind, but when you say it aloud, it should sound conversational and caring. Your intention will shine through, even if your words are not quite accurate.

The best way to learn about *short list reflections* is to practice them. Following are two sets of exercises to get you started. You can then go out and practice these reflections in real interactions with people, with or without conflict.

Listening is among the most generous ways to give. When a loved one talks to us – whether their words appear to be deep or shallow – listen. For in some way, they are baring their souls.

—Jan Karon,
American novelist

Exercise 5.1   Make a List—I

[Duration: about ten minutes]

All four exercises here make up one conversation. Read each of the following SPEAKER paragraphs and then write a LISTENER short list reflection. There are a variety of statements you could make in response to the speaker's statements, and you may or may not want an intro or outro comment; it depends on what feels natural to you. The first exercise is filled in to help you get the hang of it. Check out the following pages to help you analyze your responses.

1. SPEAKER: "Don't even tell me you tried calling me! I've got a cell phone and I can see there has been no call! So not only don't you call me, then you lie about it! This is crazy-making for me! You always do this! Ooh, I don't even know what to do!"

    LISTENER: Intro: <u>OK, hang on. I want to make sure I get it.</u>

    List: <u>I didn't call you.</u>
    <u>Then I lied about it</u>
    <u>and I do this all the time.</u>
    <u>This makes you feel crazy.</u>

    Outro: <u>Is there more?</u>

2. SPEAKER: "Whenever we get together, you're always late. You act as if my time isn't important and just arrive whenever you feel like it. Do you know how disrespectful that is?"

    LISTENER: Intro: _____

    List: _____
    _____
    _____
    _____

    Outro: _____

3. SPEAKER: "I try to be patient but I really get my feelings hurt." [sigh] "I'm sorry I sounded so mean, but I've really had it. You're not *always* late, but often you are. And why the heck are you lying to me anyway? I just can't figure out why you told me you called when you didn't."

    LISTENER: Intro: _____

    List: _____

    _____

    _____

    _____

    Outro: _____

4. SPEAKER: "Well, I really want to hear what you have to say. You haven't said what's going on for you!"

    LISTENER: Intro: _____

    List: _____

    _____

    _____

    _____

    Outro: _____

Exercise 5.1   Make a List—I

Let's Try It Together

Your answers may look different, but here are some ideas for how the Gesture looks using *short list reflections*:

1. SPEAKER: "Don't even tell me you tried calling me! I've got a cell phone and I can see there has been no call! Not only don't you call me, then you lie about it! This is crazy-making for me! You always do this! Ooh, I don't even know what to do."

    LISTENER: Intro: <u>OK, hang on. I want to make sure I get it.</u>

    List: <u>I didn't call you.</u>

    <u>Then I lied about it</u>

    <u>and I do this all the time.</u>

    <u>This makes you feel crazy.</u>

    Outro: <u>Is there more?</u>

2. SPEAKER: "Whenever we get together you're always late. You act as if my time isn't important and just arrive whenever you feel like it. Do you know how disrespectful that is?"

    LISTENER: Intro: <u>[None]</u>

    List: <u>I'm always late</u>

    <u>and that really disrespects you!</u>

    Outro: <u>[Silence]</u>

   *Notice that the listener does not answer the question. It appears rhetorical and answering it would take the focus away from the speaker.

3. SPEAKER: "I try to be patient but I really get my feelings hurt." [sigh] "I'm sorry I sounded so mean, but I've really had it. You're not *always* late, but often you are. And why the heck are you lying to me anyway? I just can't figure out why you would not call me and pretend that you did. I can't make sense of it."

LISTENER: Intro: <u>OK.</u>

List: <u>The phone thing has you really confounded</u>
<u>and I'm late pretty often.</u>
<u>I'm lying to you</u>
<u>and you're *really* hurt.</u>

Outro: <u>Is there more?</u>

*Notice the listener doesn't jump to an apology, but continues going to the heat.

4. SPEAKER: "Well, I really want to hear what you have to say. You haven't said what's going on for you."

LISTENER: <u>I'd like to talk, too, but before I do, I'm working on doing good</u>
<u>listening.</u>
<u>I'd like to make sure you get heard out.</u>
<u>Is there more?</u>

*The transparency of the listener here is important since the speaker is likely to notice this new behavior.

> The truth is that our finest moments are most likely to occur when we are feeling deeply uncomfortable, unhappy or unfulfilled. For it is only in such moments, propelled by our discomfort, that we are likely to step out of our ruts and start searching for different ways or truer answers.
>
> —M. Scott Peck,
> *The Road Less Traveled*

Exercise 5.2   Make a List—II

[Duration: about ten minutes]

More practice! This is a conversation. Read each of the following SPEAKER paragraphs and then write a LISTENER reflection in short list form.

1. SPEAKER: "What's going on here? I leave town for five days and this house is a wreck! And nothing on the to-do list is done. Aargh! I knew this would happen. You are completely irresponsible."

    LISTENER: Intro: _____

    List: _____

    _____

    _____

    _____

    Outro: _____

2. SPEAKER: "It's not just a mess, things are destroyed! I just saw my favorite vase in the trash. The dishes are piled up. And there are flies everywhere."

    LISTENER: Intro: _____

    List: _____

    _____

    _____

    _____

    Outro: _____

3. SPEAKER: "No, that's really it. I guess not everything is destroyed. It's really the vase. I feel so upset about that old vase."

   LISTENER: Intro: _____

   List: _____

   _____

   _____

   _____

   Outro: _____

4. SPEAKER: "Actually I never liked the vase. Wasn't it horrid? But it was my mom's and I felt a responsibility to have it out. Ha! Good riddance!"

People, if you pay attention to them, change the direction of one another's conversations constantly. It's like having a passenger in your car who suddenly grabs the steering wheel and turns you down a side street.

—Garth Stein,
The Art of Racing in the Rain

Exercise 5.2   Make a List—II

Let's Try It Together

1. SPEAKER: "What's going on here? I leave town for five days and this house is
    a wreck! And nothing on the to-do list is done. Aargh! I knew this would
    happen. You are completely irresponsible."

    LISTENER: Intro: <u>Ooh, hang on!</u>

            List: <u>I'm unreliable!</u>

                   <u>Nothing got done</u>

                   <u>and everything's a mess.</u>

          Outro: [None]

2. SPEAKER: "It's not just a mess, things are destroyed! I just saw my favorite vase in
    the trash. The dishes are piled up. And there are flies everywhere."

    LISTENER: Intro: <u>So,</u>

            List: <u>there are flies everywhere</u>

                   <u>and there are dirty dishes in the sink</u>

                   <u>and I broke your mom's vase.</u>

          Outro: <u>Is there more?</u>

3. SPEAKER: "No, that's really it. I guess not everything is destroyed. It's really the
    vase. I feel so upset about that old vase."

    LISTENER: Intro: [None]

            List: <u>It's a bummer about the vase.</u>

          Outro: [None]

*Notice the listener doesn't jump to reflect that the speaker had overstated how
wrecked everything was. The listener sticks with reflecting what is bothering the
speaker so that they can feel listened to.

4. SPEAKER: "Actually I never liked the vase. Wasn't it horrid? But it was my mom's
    and I felt a responsibility to have it out. Ha! Good riddance!"

You can see from the exercises that the speaker calms down soon after feeling listened to. Although their upsetness may reappear during the conversation, it is indeed common for people to calm down quickly when they are given recognition. We are not merely nodding our heads and saying, "Uh-huh, uh-huh," we are making sure that the speaker *really* feels that we understand and that we care.

Exercise 5.3　Live Practice

[Duration: five minutes each]

1. Find a family member or a friend to do this exercise with you.

2. Ask them to begin with one of the following inflammatory statements and then to continue to role play the scenario. (You are also welcome to come up with your own real or pretend scenarios.) Ask them to be as upset as possible and let them know that you don't have any expectation of taking on the speaking role, even if your scenario is real.

3. Choose a scenario, use the *Tell Me More Gesture* to give the speaker the feeling of getting listened to, and do it until they are all the way done.

4. When you are done with the scenario, ask your speaker how it felt to them and note your own feelings during the process. Write these down in Journal Exercise 5.1.

5. Do this *at least* two more times with the same or different speaker.

Inflammatory Statements

- You're completely selfish. You only think of yourself!
- You are not welcome here anymore. You have taken advantage of me for the last time!
- You're a control freak! Everyone knows it!
- You're a lazy slob! All you ever do is sit on that couch and watch TV.
- You've spoken to me like that for the last time! I'm not going to put up with your abuse anymore.

Fine-Tuning Your Reflections

Here are more thoughts on how you can gain proficiency at the Gesture. With practice, they will add authenticity and depth to your reflections.

1. The unfinished sentence
2. Three do-not-use phrases
3. Speaking without boundaries
4. Timing
5. The temptation to fix
6. Know your intention
7. Just begin it

1. The Unfinished Sentence

Before going to a party I just tell myself to listen with affection to anyone who talks to me, to be in their shoes when they talk; to try to know them without my mind pressing against theirs, or arguing, or changing the subject. No. My attitude is, "Tell me more."

—Brenda Ueland,
Strength to Your Sword Arm

You have learned about the two main types of reflections for the *Tell Me More Gesture*, quick phrases and short lists. Notice that the essence of both types is *quick* and *short*. Our job is to give the speaker the feeling of getting listened to and then get out of the way so that they can continue on. There is another type of reflection that is useful and effective, although it is to be used less often. I call it the *unfinished sentence*.

The unfinished sentence is when you begin a sentence, then pause and purposefully wait for the speaker to fill in the blank. Here are some ideas of phrases to use:

✓ So you're really . . . [blank].

✓ It sounds like you're . . . [blank].

✓ This experience has been really . . . [blank].

The unfinished sentence is truly opening up the conversation. Notice that the unfinished sentences are *not* anything like these:

✗ So you did that because . . . [blank].

✗ You are upset because . . . [blank].

✗ Your part in this is . . . [blank].

While these statements might appear open, they are actually directive because they are leading the speaker to give specific information or to take perspective. They have a subtly manipulative feel to them.

Example: The unfinished sentence

Inflammatory statement: "You are the most self-absorbed person in the whole world! I can't take it anymore!"

Good reflection: "I'm completely self-absorbed!" [quick phrase reflection]

Speaker: "Yes, you are! You only think of yourself!"

Good reflection: "You've really had it! Tell me more!" [quick phrase reflection]

Speaker: "Well, I will! You've used me up. You've taken advantage of my good nature and now I'm done. I'm not going to take it anymore. You are a complete narcissist."

Good reflection: "OK. I'm a narcissist. I've taken advantage
                 of you. And now you're done. Really done. Is
                 there more?" [short list reflection]
Speaker: "Is there more? Of course there's more! You
              obviously have no idea!"
Not-so-good reflection: "So this is really difficult because . . ."
                 [unfinished sentence]
Good reflection: [leaning in] "Whoa, this is really . . ."
                 [unfinished sentence]
Speaker: [sigh] "Miserable. I'm miserable."
[And so on.]

Coaching note: Notice that the listener does not jump to use the unfinished sentence reflection right away. The scenario plays out and then the unfinished sentence is a genuine attempt to find out what is going on for the speaker. The good reflection is truly an opening for the speaker to say absolutely anything while the not-so-good reflection is a specific question for information. Check out this story:

■ ■ ■

Josh was reflecting to Melanie during a private workshop in my office. She had been struggling with his (perceived) lack of empathy about her troubles with her aging mother. Josh was leaning forward and reflecting what he had been hearing. He said statements such as, "You've had it! She's driving you nuts," or "She calls you all the time demanding your attention." Melanie was visibly distressed and, although Josh was trying, she was not feeling satisfied. Since this was a workshop (not a mediation), I called a momentary timeout and suggested to Josh that he try the *unfinished sentence*. He turned to her, leaned way in, slowly nodded his head, and very slowly said, "Wow. You're really . . ." and as if I had written her script, Melanie piped right in and with a huge sigh of relief said, "Exhausted!" And then she sobbed. Josh was silent as he just sat with her. He took her hand and held it. Melanie then picked up her head, looked right at Josh, and continued, "I'm completely exhausted. I can't think straight. I don't have any energy for anyone. Not for you, not for me, not for the kids. I'm a failure."

■   ■   ■

What happened here is not atypical. Melanie got clear that (at least part of) what was distressing her was that she was exhausted and felt like a failure. Josh had offered a genuine and empathic opening that helped her assess what was truly upsetting her. When we sincerely try to open up the conversation, rather than try to control it, the results are astonishing. Note that Josh's tone and body language exuded his intention to deeply understand what was going on for Melanie. Using the *unfinished sentence* requires this sincerity, so that the speaker feels free to be honest, and perhaps vulnerable, to speak their truth.

> In the middle of difficulty lies opportunity.
>
> —Albert Einstein, German-born physicist

2. Three do-not-use phrases

As listeners, there are three phrases that we use in our everyday conflict conversations that are *not* productive. If we could strike these from our repertoires of conflict conversation, we would all be better off.

Do Not Say	Why?
I feel that way, too.	This is minimizing and brings the focus back to you, the listener, instead of keeping it on the speaker. This might feel like you are providing empathy, but you are actually diminishing the impact of the speaker's upsetness by telling them about your own feelings.
Well, you do that, too.	This is the what's-good-for-the-goose-is-good-for-the-gander defense and it is not part of the Gesture. Even if you are being criticized for something that the speaker does and you see irony in their statements, this is their time to speak. It is your job, if you decide you are committed to the Gesture, to make sure they feel listened to. This is a great opportunity to use the *safety net statement*, "Tell me more."
I understand.	This sounds more like you're trying to shut someone up than trying to give them the feeling of getting listened to. If you want them to know that you understand you need to say what it is exactly that you understand—otherwise it sounds, and perhaps is, phony or presumptuous. You might try saying, "Oh, I think I understand now. You're saying . . ." This is validating to

the speaker and gives them the opportunity to clarify. Or you can skip all the qualifiers and just make a *short list reflection* of what it is that you understand.

3. Speaking without boundaries

The goal of the Gesture is to encourage the speaker to speak without boundaries. You as the listener are devoted to deep listening because you understand that when people are upset, they may very well act upset. Believe it or not, people who are angry, lashing out, or ranting have many good attributes. They are engaged. They are sensitive. They are attempting to communicate. They feel passionate about a topic or situation. When we put boundaries on people who are upset about how they should speak, what words are acceptable, how loud they may talk, what topics are out of bounds, or how they should feel or react, we stifle the potential for getting to the bottom of what is really bothering them. If someone is willing to communicate, let's not stop them.

> I don't believe in critical listening, for that only puts a person in a straightjacket of hesitancy. He begins to choose his words solemnly or primly. His little inner fountain cannot spring. Critical listeners dry you up.
>
> —Brenda Ueland,
> *Strength to Your Sword Arm*

Imagine that there are no rules about what to say or how to say it. Then, as listeners, we accept anything the speaker delivers. We are not thinking critically, we are accepting. We are not judging the grammar, nor the logic or lack of logic, nor the order in which the thoughts are presented. We do not require someone to be eloquent. We only encourage them to express

> **We do not ask them to please us by accommodating us — we demonstrate that it will please us if they present their genuine self.**

themselves in a way that is authentic. They are free to make mistakes. They are free to be emotional. We are not asking them to please us by accommodating us—we demonstrate that it will please us if they present their genuine self.

Allowing someone to speak without boundaries makes a huge impact on the course of a conversation. When we welcome the speaker to expound in an authentic manner, the outcome, often the transformation, is astounding. Thích Nhất Hanh (2011) wrote, "You must love in such a way that the person you love feels free." (page 4) We can apply this to the art of reflection and say, "You must listen in such a way that the speaker feels free." This is the essence of the *Tell Me More Gesture*.

> You must listen in such a way that the speaker feels free.

4. Timing

The more heated or inflammatory the comments, the more often you should be reflecting. This can feel like you are putting your head in the lion's mouth, but it is exactly what is called for. When my mediation clients are having a productive conversation where they are listening to each other and feeling listened to, there is rarely a need for my intervention. But when they are upset, I sit forward and reflect often, which is good support.

The same goes for a conversation without a third party helper. When the speaker is more conversational and relaxed, you may choose to listen for long periods without reflecting. When the conversation heats up, this is when you sit forward, say, "Tell me more," and make reflections more often. As listeners, we are continually deciding what will provide the most support for the speaker.

5.   The temptation to fix

Let's just admit that we all do it: We fix. When attempting to be an incredible listener with good intentions to give the feeling of getting listened to—not to give advice but just to be present for the speaker's needs—we all abandon ship at some point and say something to help fix the problem or the person. It is completely natural, because we think we can shortcut a discussion or a problem; we *truly* want to help.

Fixing comes in a lot of different disguises, including giving information, clarifying, advising, problem solving, and apologizing. All of these are subtle and not-so-subtle ways of trying to get the speaker to stop talking. All of these methods of fixing also indicate that we as the listener assume that the speaker needs our help.

How to stop fixing: The first thing to do is to recognize that, as the listener, this is *our* panic. This is our need to be a helper. We are fulfilling our own need to *do* something based on our own discomfort with the situation. When we move to fix or help, not only are we shutting them down, we actually might be disrespecting the person by making the assumption that they need help. We are no longer doing deep listening if, in our minds or in our statements, we are problem solving.

Once you recognize your impulse to start problem solving, the second thing to do is to rely on the *safety net phrases* and say, "Tell me more," until the impulse passes. This keeps you from jumping to conclusions about the speaker's needs and allows you to wring out the washcloth so that they can be listened to until they are all-the-way done.

6. Know your intention

The crux of the matter is that if you know, in the moment, what your intention is when you make a reflection, you can make better choices for what to say. That is, you must be extremely self-aware and mindful of your purpose for making a reflection. Here are some great reasons to make a reflection:

To listen more.
To understand better.
To clarify.
To show empathy.
To open up the conversation.

Here are some not-so-good reasons to make a reflection:

To pin them down.
To calm them down.
To make them be logical.
To make them stop talking.
To prove them wrong.
To defend yourself.
To make them get to the point.

Remember that regardless of the exact words you choose to make a reflection, your overall gesture will send a strong message about your intentions. If you appear genuinely interested in hearing more, then the speaker is likely to feel that intention.

> Paradoxically, admitting your own powerlessness can free you from the need to fix everything and allow us to be truly present to the other person, and to listen. A cartoon in The New Yorker had one woman saying testily to her friend, 'There's no point in our being friends if you won't let me fix you.
>
> —James Martin,
> *The Jesuit Guide
> to (Almost) Everything*

7. Just begin it

If you have known the speaker for twenty days or twenty years, you can begin it. If you have tried discussing the topic for a minute or for a year, you can begin it. If you just said something really rude or if you have sat there silently, you can begin it. If you are partners, workmates, schoolmates, or perfect strangers, you can begin it. Once it occurs to you, you can change your tack completely, and just begin it.

This might sound obvious, but the truth is that many people do not start it because they believe it is too late, that they have missed their opportunity. It is a subject that is too hot or too old, or they have already behaved in a way that isn't within the ideals of the Gesture. That's OK, just begin it. And when the speaker says to you, "You're just doing that method you were telling me about," you respond, "Yes! I just remembered. I really want to listen to you. Please do tell me more."

■ ■ ■

Hannah was a workshop attendee who was extremely interested in the Gesture but also was struggling with how exactly to utilize it. It felt in sync with her values, but she also felt some nervousness about beginning it. Toward the end of our second of two workshops together, Hannah had an *aha!* moment. Sitting in our small circle, she suddenly exclaimed, "I can do this with anyone! A friend, for example. When the back and forth starts, I can start the Gesture!"

■   ■   ■

Exactly. When it occurs to you, you begin it. Whenever you have the impulse, begin it. Lean forward and say, "Tell me more," and you will have already begun. The speaker will indeed tell you more.

Moving Forward

In chapter 5 we explored the second type of reflection, the *short list reflection*, for when the speaker is still upset but is talking in sentences and providing information. We discussed that there are many attributes of good reflections to help fulfill the *Tell Me More Gesture*, but it is important to not get hamstrung with rules so you can feel free to be yourself and be an attentive, responsive listener. It will be helpful to try on one concept at a time and practice it at nonconflict times. Knowing your intention will help you make good reflections that will help open up the speaker to feel free to, indeed, tell you more. Before you move on, please accomplish the following journal entries. These are an important part of the learning and skill-building process.

Journal Entry 5.1

In Exercise 5.3 (page 107), you practiced the Gesture with volunteer speakers. Did the speaker feel free to continue? Did the speaker move toward clarity and calmness? For you as the listener, what worked well and what felt awkward?

_____

_____

_____

_____

_____

_____

_____

_____

_____

_____

_____

_____

_____

_____

_____

_____

_____

Journal Entry 5.2

You have been given a lot of information in the first five chapters of *The Tell Me More Gesture*. What makes the most sense to you so far? What rings true? What concepts are most confusing or difficult?

_____

_____

_____

_____

_____

_____

_____

_____

_____

_____

_____

_____

_____

_____

_____

Chapter 6:
RESERVING JUDGMENT

Saying "Tell me more" and making effective reflections when someone is upset with you is easy to talk about, but not so easy to accomplish. The key to success in the *Tell Me More Gesture* is to become aware of our inner reactions during conflict. In any situation, regular or conflict, there is a range of possible reactions, from judgment to empathy.

> When you are in psychological distress and someone really hears you without passing judgment on you, without trying to take responsibility for you, without trying to mold you, it feels damn good!
>
> —Carl Rogers,
> *A Way of Being*

Judgment	Curiosity	Empathy
Assessment	Interest	Care
Discernment	Wonder	Compassion
Preference		Kindness

Judgment, curiosity, and empathy—each of these reactions is appropriate at different moments in our lives. The most productive, connecting reaction in any conflict situation is empathy, yet it is also the most difficult to achieve.

Judgment is the forming of an opinion or criticizing someone from a position of assumed moral superiority. Another way of thinking about judgment is that it is merely one forming an opinion by discerning and comparing. Assessment, discernment, and preference all fall under the heading of judgment. Know that when someone is upset, and the listener reacts with any of the definitions of judgment, it *feels* like assumed superiority to the speaker, even though the speaker's intention may be different. When you disagree with someone during a heated conflict, this is what judgment feels like to them:

> People who judge others tell more about Who They Are, than Who They Judge.
>
> —Donald Hicks,
> *Look Into Stillness*

Judgment during conflict:
*I disagree, and I condemn you for
thinking that way.*

Curiosity is the strong desire to know or learn something. Wonder and interest are similar. You can disagree with someone and still be curious about what is going on for them. Curiosity has an openness to it that is refreshing because it lacks judgment. During a conflict or disagreement, curiosity feels like this to the other person:

Curiosity during conflict:
*I disagree, but I'm interested in knowing
why you think that way.*

Empathy is the ability to understand and share the feelings of another. Compassion, care, and kindness are not exactly empathy, but they come under the heading of empathy because they radiate a similar warmth and a welcoming nature. Empathy, during a difficult discussion or disagreement, feels like this to the other person:

Empathy during conflict:
I know what it feels like to feel that way.

Being judgmental destroys the connection that we crave, yet we are all wired to make judgments. Discerning, assessing, decision-making, developing preferences—they all require judgment. These are necessary skills in everyday life. Obviously, we should not completely stop judgment, but we do need to reserve it in order to be most successful during conflicts.

Notice that when we use empathy, we do not communicate whether we disagree or not, although it is often implicit during a conflict that the participants disagree. The *Tell Me More Gesture*, at its highest level, means that we do not express our thoughts. This is not a time when we expect to be heard; we are not concerned with being understood. We want the speaker to receive the feeling of being deep-down listened to. Therefore, we don't communicate our own opinions or feelings in any way.

> If we could read the secret history of our enemies, we should find in each man's life sorrow and suffering enough to disarm all hostility.
>
> —Henry Wadsworth Longfellow, American poet

Reserving judgment means more than simply not expressing the judgment. It means that, at least temporarily, we suspend any judgments that we are thinking. We decide to simply believe the speaker. We must become conscious of where the judgments come from and put them on hold. When we reserve judgment, we buy into these four concepts:

The Four Basics to Reserving Judgment

1. There is no such thing as an absolute truth.
2. We all have bias.
3. The (so-called) facts don't matter.
4. Receive and believe.

Let's look at these individually.

1.   There is no such thing as an absolute truth.

An absolute truth is an inflexible reality—something that is *always* true. Believing that something is always true is an impediment to being able to take the perspective of another. While something *feels* like a truth, it is actually a judgment, no matter how firmly you believe the truth to be universal. There is no such thing as an absolute truth. (Notice the irony of stating this concept in this manner, which demonstrates the concept itself since the statement is inflexible.) The point is that we need to let go of anything that we believe is a hard and fast truth. This includes many concepts, such as:

acceptable versus unacceptable,
appropriate versus inappropriate,
beautiful versus ugly,

> To love a man enough to help him, you have to forfeit the warm, self-righteous glow that comes from judging.
>
> —Ron Hall,
> *Same Kind of Different as Me*

delicious versus tasteless,

fun versus boring,

good versus bad,

helpful versus unhelpful,

loud versus quiet,

right versus wrong,

smart versus stupid,

true versus false,

and so on.

> If you are not wrong, then you will be willing to consider how you might be mistaken.
>
> —The Arbinger Institute, *The Anatomy of Peace*

Many times we are certain that a person is beautiful, that a sound was loud, that a shrug was dismissive, and so on. To reserve judgment you believe that there is always another side, another way of thinking. Think about it: Even hot versus cold is a judgment. Some people love their coffee extremely hot. I like hot coffee, but scalding hot beverages burn my mouth. How is it that that which burns me doesn't burn someone else? It seems that even hot versus cold is a judgment.

> The stronger our preferences, the more we are tempted to hold them high as truths.

Reserving judgment is an ongoing practice of deciding that our preferences are just that: preferences. The stronger they are, the more we are tempted to hold them high as truths. I often think to myself, *It will do me no harm to listen and wait while I undertake to understand him more deeply.* So the crux here is to understand that there is no right or wrong. There is no ultimate truth.

2. We all have bias.

The next step in reserving judgment is to realize that, even though we are intelligent beings, we all have biases. Biases serve to limit our ability to make rational judgments and decisions. Biases are mistakes that keep us from being fully rational.

We know about gender, ethnicity, age, religious, sexual orientation, and many other social biases and stereotypes. Following are some biases you may not have considered (Noba n.d.).

Overconfidence: having greater certainty in your judgment than is rationally warranted.

Framing: the way something is presented to you affects your judgment.

Bounded willpower: giving greater concern to present concerns over those in the future.

So what's the lesson here? We all have biases simply because we are human. We are all faulty in our ability to make decisions and judgments. Therefore, when you are certain of something, *especially* when you are certain, it is an opportunity to remind yourself that there is always room for another view. You must question your own judgment and momentarily set it aside. You can think to yourself, *I am certain about this, but I know I have biases.*

3. The (so-called) facts don't matter.

An important aspect to reserving judgment is letting go of fact-finding. Facts are somewhat like truths and, contrary to your intuition, can get in the way of a good discussion for two reasons. First, facts are nearly always disputable. And second, facts don't matter when you are attempting to truly listen to another person's story, perception, or truth.

> For every fact there is an infinity of hypotheses.
>
> —Robert M. Pirsig,
> *Zen and the Art of
> Motorcycle Maintenance*

Mediation participants rarely arrive in my office with the same set of facts. They either view the same event differently or they pluck out different (so-called) facts from their history to explain their own experience. In the end, it is usually not the facts that matter most, as in the following story of these mediation clients:

■   ■   ■

Sofia and Gary, never married, had been together fifteen years and, after a long history of battling and fighting, they had decided to call it quits. They were dealing with the issue of figuring out how much equity in the house each deserved after owning it for only a year and a half. Gary had put a lot of money into the house as well as labor, and Sofia, being a skilled electrician, had put many hours of labor into the electricity and plumbing. Gary would say, "I used the equity from the previous house I owned to buy this house. And there's almost no real equity in this house since we bought it so recently." One point for Gary. Sofia would say, "I put in an enormous number of hours of my time to accomplish projects you would have paid an arm and a leg for." One point for Sofia.

■ ■ ■

They did not dispute each other's facts because they were both right. Both of the facts were true. Of course, there were many more facts, but in the end, it didn't come down to the facts. It came down to them hearing each other more deeply—about Sofia putting loving time into a place she figured she would grow old in; about Gary working hard not only financially supporting them as a couple, but also physically giving his own time and labor; and about the hurt feelings they had from the way they treated each other.

> Still, what I want in my life Is to be willing to be dazzled –
> to cast aside the weight of facts and maybe even to float a little above this difficult world.
>
> —Mary Oliver,
> *"The Ponds", House of Light*

In other cases, I have seen that people go through an experience together and come out with completely different facts. "It was two years ago." "No, three years ago." "He was rude." "No, he wasn't." "You shoved me." "No, I was defending myself." "I was trying to help." "No, you're just nosy." And so on.

■ ■ ■

In 2016, I witnessed and videoed a white police officer grabbing an African American pedestrian by the back of the jacket and detaining him. A heated exchange ensued, including the pedestrian being irate and using profanities. I posted the video on YouTube, and it proceeded to go viral, being viewed by over 750,000 people. I was amazed by the range of facts that surfaced from the four thousand people who took the time to comment. This appeared to not be merely about bias, which certainly came into play. This had to do with people's views on how you should treat authority, their ability to notice minute details in the video, their ability to remember accurately, etc.

■ ■ ■

The video experience has reinforced in me the concept that there are rarely hard and fast facts. This notion has become a huge asset to me. My facts, my truth about my marriage, about my relationships with my children, about my family of origin, are certainly just that: mine. If I can let go of my facts and listen in a different way, with empathy, in the end, the one who benefits most is me.

Details and (so-called) facts are more important to some people than others, and thus, letting go of fact-finding, albeit temporarily, will be more difficult for some people. For example, people with Jungian preferences (Myers and Myers 1980) of "thinker" or "judger" might have a greater need to know details and facts than those with "feeler" or "perceiver" preferences. Please know that a greater or lesser need to know the facts of a situation is not a positive or negative trait, but it may make this particular aspect of reserving judgment more challenging. If you find the idea of letting go of facts daunting, give the following exercise a try.

> In any encounter, we have a choice: we can strengthen our resentment or our understanding and empathy. We can widen the gap between ourselves and others or lessen it.
>
> Pema Chödrön,
> American Tibetan Buddhist

> ### Exercise 6.1   Letting Go of the Facts
>
> [Duration: two minutes]
>
> In any conversation during your regular day, instead of asking specific fact-finding questions, try simply saying, "Tell me more." Here are some examples of questions we often ask when we are looking for facts when we could be listening and showing interest in a more open way. When you try this, notice if the speaker reacts favorably.
>
> | SPEAKER: | LISTENER: |
> |---|---|
> | "I got in really late last night." | Instead of: "What time was it?" |
> | | Try: "Tell me more." |
> | "I've been running all day today!" | Instead of: "Where were you?" |
> | | Try: "Tell me more." |
> | "I was so rude to a clerk today." | Instead of: "Why did you do that?" |
> | | Try: "Tell me more." |
> | "You should've seen my sister!" | Instead of: "What was she wearing?" |
> | | Try: "Tell me more." |
> | "The boy was too old to be acting that way." | Instead of: "How old was he?" |
> | | Try: "Tell me more." |
> | "I only work two days a week." | Instead of: "What do you do?" |
> | | Try: "Tell me more about yourself." |
> | "I hate it when children yell in airplanes." | Instead of: "Do you have children?" |
> | | Try: "Tell me more." |

Once you practice this exercise a few times, you will understand that when you let go of fact finding, one of two things likely will happen: (1) your question will get answered without your needing to ask, or (2) the speaker will take the conversation in a direction that will make your original question unnecessary or obsolete. When you practice the Gesture, you may become more comfortable with not asking for specific information and more intrigued with whatever information the speaker wants to provide. This helps you find out more about them in a deeper way. Might you ultimately want to ask a question or two? Yes, perhaps, but you will have heard the speaker, and the speaker will have experienced you, in a different, more open way.

> **When you practice the Gesture, you may become more comfortable with not asking for specific information and more intrigued with information the speaker wants to provide.**

4. Receive and believe

The essence of reserving judgment during a conflict is to *receive and believe*. Receive and believe means that we trust that the speaker means what they say. We simply receive the communication and believe it. No matter how ridiculous, convoluted, or untrue the statements seem, we decide to give the person the feeling of getting listened to and to do so until they are all-the-way done. The result is that you maintain a positive connection with the speaker during their distress, which will result in them gaining clarity and feeling connected to you.

While you might be wondering why the speaker feels the way they do and how they got to that place, you don't ask, nor do you require them to prove anything. You say, "Tell me more." Requiring proof is a defensive response, virtually the same as a judgmental response, but with an attempt to feign curiosity. This sort of manipulation, intentional or not, is not consistent with the Gesture. You can think to yourself, *There is a good reason for the speaker to be in this place, to have these feelings. I don't need to quiz them; I can just believe them.*

Think about this: How do *you* feel when someone is judging you? Do you feel self-conscious? Are you likely to be your most open, most eloquent self? No. Consciously or unconsciously, you change your behavior as a result of the judgmental feedback you are receiving. You might try to be more pleasing or you might get defensive and stand your ground more firmly. You might sound nicer, meaner, quieter, louder—whatever the result, it is a different one than if you had received an empathic response. The speaker must feel welcome to be authentic.

When you receive and believe, you think to yourself, *We disagree and that's OK.* If you say this to yourself when you are feeling judgmental (and when you may be feeling judged yourself), then you will be well on your way to reserving judgment. This will not only help you accomplish the *Tell Me More Gesture*, but also it will help reduce your own stress. Being judgmental is a stressor on you emotionally and physically. You will feel better as you learn to judge less. Here is some practice for you:

Exercise 6.2 We Disagree

[Duration: two minutes]

Read aloud each of the speaker's statements below as if someone were saying them to you (pretend that you disagree if you do not), and then say very softly to yourself, "We disagree and that's OK." Notice that the further you go in the list, the more personal the statements become, *and* you can still think, *We disagree and that's OK.*

SPEAKER:	YOU:
"I hate marshmallows."	We disagree and that's OK.
"I love hiking."	We disagree and that's OK.
"I make the best apple pie."	We disagree and that's OK.
"That painting is ugly."	We disagree and that's OK.
"I love horror films."	We disagree and that's OK.
"You play too many video games."	We disagree and that's OK.
"Your jewelry is gaudy."	We disagree and that's OK.
"You are a horrible person."	We disagree and that's OK.

Letting go of judgment is the first step every single time you are in a conflict. Whether the disagreement is large or small, "We disagree and that's OK" is the beginning of reserving your judgment about the speaker so that you can open yourself up to new information and a more positive conflict interaction.

Know that you can use other similar statements to help yourself from judging others, even when you are not in a conflict or perhaps when you meet a perfect stranger. We all have prejudices and judgments that we learned when we were very young, and we can practice letting go of them by thinking to ourselves statements such as:

> We're different and that's OK.
> We grew up differently and that's OK.
> We look different and that's OK.

We talk differently and that's OK.

Different things are important to you and that's OK.

If Exercise 6.2 is difficult for you, you may want to think about what it is inside you that is keeping you from letting go of judgments. (See chapter 8, "Get Hold of Yourself.")

Moving Forward

In chapter 6 you learned that reserving judgment is absolutely essential to good conflict communication. Being able to think and believe *We disagree and that's OK* is perhaps the second most important aspect to the Gesture, the most important being to lean forward and say, "Tell me more." Nothing enflames a conflict more than judgment. Before moving on to the next chapter, please spend about fifteen minutes reflecting on and completing the two journal exercises.

Journal Entry 6.1

On page 124-125, there is a list of topics that people often hold as absolute truths. Choose one or two from the list and write a paragraph for each about why you feel (at least somewhat) justified making judgments about those topics.

_____

_____

_____

_____

_____

_____

_____

_____

_____

_____

_____

_____

_____

_____

_____

_____

_____

_____

Journal Entry 6.2

Look back at your response to Journal Entry 2.2 (page 46). How have your thoughts about the Gesture changed? Are you finding more ease? More or different frustrations? Make some notes here about your feelings at this point regarding the *Tell Me More Gesture*.

_____

_____

_____

_____

_____

_____

_____

_____

_____

_____

_____

_____

_____

_____

_____

_____

_____

_____

Chapter 7:
FINDING EMPATHY

Now that you understand the importance of reserving judgment, and you are practiced in changing your mindset to doing so, you can learn to respond to conflict in ways that are not merely neutral or curious, but actually show empathy for the speaker. Remember, this is your opportunity to learn something new, go deeper, and keep or reestablish connection with someone while in conflict.

> No, I'm not insulted when people call me sensitive. Feeling things deeply is my super power. I'm an empathetic badass.
>
> —Nanea Hoffman,
> Sweatpants & Coffee
> online magazine

The Four Basics of an Empathic Response

The first step to changing our conflict responses to empathy is to understand what an empathic response looks like. Here are some basics:

1. Have soft, welcoming body language.

During a session in my office, a man told his wife, whom he was experiencing as judgmental, that he was looking for a soft place to land. I noted at the time that this is a wonderful expression for what it feels like to receive empathy. So what is welcoming body language? Warm eyes, a slight tilt of the head, a bit of nodding, a thoughtful expression, a slightly upturned mouth, leaning forward—all of these are ways that you, without saying anything, can demonstrate to the speaker that you are listening and that you care.

2. Make reflective statements; don't ask questions.

Questions sound curious, but can also sound like an examination or a judgment—as if something needs to be proven. It might feel to you that asking for more information sounds as if you are truly interested, for example, "How did this happen?" or "Why do you feel that way?" But a simple, "Oh no! Tell me more," is preferable in conflict situations.

3. Name something that you can relate to.

Can you always find something in the speaker's experience that you have experienced yourself? Yes, you can. You can say, "You were really terrified," or "What a disappointment!" or "How awful!"—all are feelings with which you can empathize. You can see that if you can't understand their exact experience, you can understand a portion of it. If you can't understand anything about their specific experience, you can understand more generally how upset they are. This is why statements such as "You've had it!" and "This is really difficult!" are so effective. They demonstrate an understanding of the speaker's underlying experience without specificity.

> The empathic listener celebrates the naturalness of what is felt – "No wonder you were mad!" – and helps to overcome the other person's tendency to hold back.
>
> —Michael P. Nichols,
> *The Lost Art of Listening*

4. Be earnest.

Know that your reflection must sound and appear (and be) earnest. This can be generated from self-interest (see *The Ten Gifts of Listening*, pages 52-53) or concern for the speaker. Without sincerity, reflections can sound condescending or presumptuous. If the speaker believes that you are listening and reflecting because you are genuinely interested and that you truly care, they will feel encouraged to tell you more.

> You never really understand a person until you consider things from his point of view.
>
> —Harper Lee,
> *To Kill a Mockingbird*

Please consider the idea that you can always find something to empathize with, even when someone is upset with you, if *you* are in a place to do so. In chapter 8, we will discuss our own barriers to making an empathic response and what to do about overcoming those barriers.

Notice that in the *four basics of an empathic response*, none of the attributes of empathy are demonstrated through curiosity. Curiosity lacks the warmth and understanding of empathy. Curiosity is not usually a harmful response, of course. It is a huge step past judgment, but it is not as effective as empathy in creating a connecting experience during times of conflict.

Meeting Judgment with Empathy

Often we feel a right to judge someone who is judging us. Perhaps we are entitled to this, but entitlement is not a good rationale when we are trying to have wholesome reactions to conflict. Many people who have taken my workshops have an initial response such as, "Well, this might work for most people, but my situation is different. It is more drastic." If you are feeling skeptical that empathy can change the course of your interactions, then you should know about the book *Not by the Sword* (1995), the true story of the Jewish cantor Michael Weisser and his wife, Julie Weisser. They were harassed by the aggressive and intimidating actions of Larry Trapp, a grand dragon of the Ku Klux Klan in Omaha, Nebraska.

■ ■ ■

The Weissers were receiving threatening mail from Larry Trapp that contained such things as "Your time is up" and "The 'Holohoax' was nothing compared to what's going to happen to you." Michael started trying to contact Larry by phone, and when he didn't answer, Michael left messages telling Larry that, when he gave up his hating, a world of love awaited him. One day, Larry suddenly decided to pick up the phone and said, "Why the f*** are you harassing me?! Stop harassing me!" Michael responded calmly, "Well, I know you're in a wheelchair and I thought maybe I could take you to the grocery store or something." Although Larry declined at the time, within a few days, the Weissers went to Larry's apartment, where they were met at the door by Larry, in a wheelchair with an automatic weapon slung over the door and a Nazi flag hung on the wall behind him. Michael shook Larry's hand and Larry began flinging off his swastika rings, saying that he couldn't wear them anymore. After the Weissers' visit, Larry Trapp renounced the Klan and got rid of his hate propaganda. "They showed me such love that I couldn't help but love them back," he said. "It's just an experience I've never had before" (Watterson 1995).

■ ■ ■

You can see that one can choose to not meet judgment with judgment, even in extreme situations. A life-changing outcome such as the Weissers and Trapp experienced is not guaranteed, but you can expect to have much improved conflict interactions when you bring empathy to a difficult conversation.

> **You can expect to have much improved conflict interactions when you bring empathy to a difficult conversation.**

Judgments about Our Opinions—easier skill

Sometimes when we disagree, we don't worry about it. Disagreement doesn't necessarily mean there is conflict. So changing our stance from judgment to empathy is easy when you don't take another's judgment personally. Here's an example:

> SPEAKER: "Autumn is my favorite season!"
> LISTENER (who hates autumn):
>   Judgmental: "You're crazy!"
>   Curious: "Huh. Why do you say that?"
>   Empathic: "Wow, you love it! Tell me more."

Having different opinions is usually completely acceptable and desirable. The important thing to note is that you can find an empathic response, even when you disagree. Notice here that when the speaker asks "Why," as in the curious response, the listener sounds less interested than in the empathic response. The empathic response here reflects the speaker's joy for autumn without demonstrating the listener's dislike for autumn.

> Remember every mistreatment experience shows up to give you the opportunity to learn love at a deeper level. You don't need to defend yourself because you cannot be diminished.
>
> —Kimberly Giles,
> *Choosing Clarity*

Conversations when the speaker's judgment doesn't bother you are opportunities for you to practice finding empathy, even though you disagree. If you listen carefully, you will find there are many times each day when you hear someone's opinion with which you disagree, and you might normally not respond at all. Use these times to practice finding an empathic response. Simply say, "Tell me more." You will find that doing this will help you connect in a new way.

Judgments about Our Outer Self—medium difficulty

It is more difficult to make an empathic response when we feel judged. Here are two examples of moving from judgment to empathy when feeling criticized:

> SPEAKER: "This spaghetti sauce is terrible! Did you
>   make this?"
> LISTENER:
>   Judgmental: "How can you say that? I just spent all
>   day making it!"
>   Curious: "Wow, I'm surprised that you don't like it."
>   Empathic: "Ooh, I hate eating things I don't like."

> SPEAKER: "That blouse is pretty low cut for someone
>   your age."
> LISTENER:
>   Judgmental: "Well, who are you to judge?"
>   Curious: "Really?"
>   Empathic: "Ooh, wow! Tell me more."

Note here that the judgmental listener response answers the original judgment with another judgment. While this is a common way to respond, it is both defensive and escalating. A he-started-it defense for judgment doesn't work in the *Tell Me More Gesture*. When something is difficult to hear, we instead can choose a curious (at a minimum) or empathic response.

At this point in my workshops, a participant usually asks me why they should do the Gesture. Why would they want to encourage someone to criticize them or treat them unkindly? Why should they accept someone judging them? I remind them, and now you, that I am not telling you that you *should* do this. It must come from your own desire and motivation. You may have decided to try the Gesture because nothing else has worked to help you through tough conflicts. You may have decided that you are better off when you practice the Gesture because *you* feel calmer, because *you* want to live to your values, because *you* want to maintain the connection. Whatever your mantra card (chapter 3) states, *that* is why you are doing this. Yes, the Gesture may benefit the annoying, belligerent speaker, and it is tempting to abandon the Gesture just when things get difficult, but this is exactly when it starts being most useful. So you, the listener, must remember the benefits to yourself in these very difficult times. You may not be in the mood to give the gift to the speaker, so give it to yourself.

> You may not be in the mood to give a gift to someone with whom you are in conflict – so give it to yourself.

Do the following exercise for some practice finding empathic responses to judgmental statements. (These aren't even the hard ones yet.)

Exercise 7.1   Judgment Meets Empathy

[Duration: ten minutes]

Respond to the judgmental statements below. Write down how you would normally like to respond, and then write an empathic response.

1. SPEAKER: "You talk too much."
    LISTENER:
        What I'd like to say: _____
        Empathic response: _____

2. SPEAKER: "Your outfit is completely inappropriate."
    LISTENER:
        What I'd like to say: _____
        Empathic response: _____

3. SPEAKER: "You're always late."
    LISTENER:
        What I'd like to say: _____
        Empathic response: _____

4. SPEAKER: "You're so clumsy! You've wrecked my artwork!"
    LISTENER:
        What I'd like to say: _____
        Empathic response: _____

5. SPEAKER: "Were you brought up in a barn?"
    LISTENER:
        What I'd like to say: _____
        Empathic response: _____

Exercise 7.1   Judgment Meets Empathy

Let's Try It Together

1. SPEAKER: "You talk too much."
   LISTENER:
       What I'd like to say: <u>Me? That's ridiculous. I can never get a word in edgewise.</u>
       Empathic response: <u>Wow, sounds like I'm annoying you.</u>

2. SPEAKER: "That outfit is completely inappropriate."
   LISTENER:
       What I'd like to say: <u>So who made you the fashion police?</u>
       Empathic response: <u>Oh! Sounds like I might embarrass you. Tell me more.</u>

3. SPEAKER: "You're always late!"
   LISTENER:
       What I'd like to say: <u>Well, just because you don't have a life, that doesn't mean I'm not busy.</u>
       Empathic response: <u>Ooh, I've made you wait!</u>

4. SPEAKER: "You're so clumsy! You've wrecked my artwork!"
   LISTENER:
       What I'd like to say: <u>You shouldn't leave your crap lying around all over the place.</u>
       Empathic response: <u>Oh, you worked so hard on that!</u>

5. SPEAKER: "Were you brought up in a barn?"
   LISTENER:
       What I'd like to say: <u>Yes, I was.</u>
       Empathic response: <u>My mess is really bugging you!</u>

Judgments about Our Beliefs—more difficult

> Listening is about being present, not just about being quiet. I meet others with the life I've lived, not just with my questions.
>
> —Krista Tippett,
> *Becoming Wise*

Finding empathy when someone is judging a strongly held belief is challenging. These instances tend to be about topics such as politics, religion, and social issues. The first thing to remember is, *We disagree and that's OK* (page 132). Then, in order to move to empathy, you must be able to find something in common with the speaker. Since you don't agree about the topic, you will find empathy for how deeply they feel about it (*I know what it is like to feel passionately about something*), for their bad choice of words (*I know what it feels like to lash out*), for their ugly behavior (*I know what it feels like to act in a way I might regret later*), etc. Eventually, you will be able to simply tell yourself, *Ah! I'm human, and they are human, too!* Here are a couple of examples.

SPEAKER: "[Insert politician here] is a dried up, old windbag."
LISTENER:
   Judgmental: "I disagree. You're stupid if you think that."
   Curious: "Interesting. Why do you say that?"
   Empathic:
      "You're really upset with her!" [emotion]
      "You really disagree with him!" [topic]
      "Tell me more!" [safety net]

SPEAKER: "People who believe in astrology are ruining
    the world."
LISTENER:
    Judgmental: "You are always overstating things."
    Curious: "Really? I'd like to hear more about why you feel
       that way."
    Empathic:
       "Wow! They are wrecking everything!" [topic]
       "You've had some bad experiences about this." [emotion]
       "Wow! Tell me more!" [safety net]

Check out this story:

■   ■   ■

In 2012, Sam and Darla, a couple whose children had long since moved away, came to my office for a mediation session to discuss terms of their impending divorce. As with many mediations, each participant was in a different place about the idea of getting divorced. This is common because, to be blunt, while the decision to get married takes two people, the decision to divorce takes only one person.

Darla was the less expressive of the two during the session, and it became clear that the divorce was her idea. She was further ahead of him in the process of coming to grips with getting a divorce. As the session progressed, Sam grew more and more agitated, expressing his dislike for change, when suddenly he blurted out to me, "My wife thinks marriage is supposed to be an equal partnership!" He was one foot from my face, looking straight at me. Sitting up attentively, I kept his gaze, then lowered my shoulders, shook my head slowly, and said with a great deal of empathy, "Wow, this is really hard." Sam visibly relaxed, and with a huge sigh he simply said, "Yes." After a minute of silence, Sam and Darla started having a productive, albeit difficult, conversation about how to move forward.

■   ■   ■

As the mediator, I did not want Sam to feel that I was judging him. I needed to find empathy for him even though our values are very different. I do not have the same belief system about marriage that Sam does, and I do not mind change like Sam does, so I could not use these items as a source of empathy for Sam. But I do know what it's like to get dumped—it is brutal. I also know what it's like to go through a divorce. Even when it is amicable, it is deeply disappointing—it is the loss of a dream. It was easy for me to find empathy for Sam. Honestly, I didn't have to think through all of that. I immediately thought to myself, *This is really upsetting*. I can have empathy for anybody in the whole world because I know what it's like to be extremely upset. So when I said to Sam, "Whoa, this is really hard," he could feel in my words, *I'm human too. I really understand.*

If *We disagree and that's OK* is our mantra for practicing nonjudgment, then this would be our mantra for practicing empathy:

> **I'm human, too—it's OK.**

Hold on to this idea of *I'm human, too—it's OK* while you give the following exercise a try to see if you can find empathy for someone who is cutting you down or disagreeing with ideas in which you strongly believe. Imagine how each conversation might progress if you gave them the feeling of being listened to until they were all-the-way done. Might you learn something new? Might you feel good about your part in the conversation? Would your stress level be lower?

> Listening to someone's story is a way of empowering them, of validating their intrinsic worth as a human being.
>
> —Kay Pranis,
> *A Call to Transform Justice*

> None of us is perfect. All of us make mistakes. And close relationships are a place where we're bound to make them. In fact, until we've seen someone's darkness we don't really know them.
>
> —Marianne Williamson,
> American spiritual teacher

Exercise 7.2   Empathy for More Difficult Scenarios

[Duration: ten minutes]

In this exercise, if you do not disagree strongly with the speaker's statements, you must pretend that you do. For each statement, write how you would respond, then write an empathic response. Consider how the conversation might change once you have changed your gesture to empathy.

1. SPEAKER: "Our taxes are being wasted on that? This makes me so angry!"
    LISTENER:
        What I'd like to say: _____
        Empathic response: _____

2. SPEAKER: "Male drivers are so aggressive! They always cut me off. And they don't slow down even in a snowstorm."
    LISTENER:
        What I'd like to say: _____
        Empathic response: _____

3. SPEAKER: "I can't believe how that man disrespected the police officer. He ought to be shot."
    LISTENER:
        What I'd like to say: _____
        Empathic response: _____

4. SPEAKER: "Did you see what your favorite politician did lately? Loser!"
    LISTENER:
        What I'd like to say: _____
        Empathic response: _____

5. SPEAKER: "Sheesh! Whatever happened to the separation of church and state?"
    LISTENER:
        What I'd like to say: _____
        Empathic response: _____

Exercise 7.2   Empathy for More Difficult Scenarios

Let's Try It Together

1. SPEAKER: "Our taxes are being wasted on that? This makes me so angry!"
   LISTENER:
       What I'd like to say: <u>That's hardly a waste. You're crazy!</u>
       Empathic response: <u>Wow, sounds like this is a big issue!</u>

2. SPEAKER: "Male drivers are so aggressive! They always cut me off. And they don't slow down even in a snowstorm."
   LISTENER:
       What I'd like to say: <u>Have you taken a look at your own driving lately?</u>
       Empathic response: <u>Yikes! Sounds like they're putting you in danger.</u>

3. SPEAKER: "I can't believe how that man disrespected the police officer. He ought to be shot."
   LISTENER:
       What I'd like to say: <u>You can't see that the officer was overzealous?</u>
       Empathic response: <u>He was disrespectful. Tell me more.</u>

4. SPEAKER: "Did you see what your favorite politician did lately? Loser!"
   LISTENER:
       What I'd like to say: <u>Yes! I feel proud of her.</u>
       Empathic response: <u>You're really upset!</u>

5. SPEAKER: "Sheesh! Whatever happened to the separation of church and state?"
   LISTENER:
       What I'd like to say: <u>What sort of person are you anyway?</u>
       Empathic response: <u>Wow, you're upset!</u>

Note that in #3 above, the listener says exactly what the speaker is expressing even though the listener disagrees. Nearly everyone worries that doing this will be mistaken for agreement. I challenge you to try it, and see what happens. My experience, professionally and personally, is that an empathic reflection being mistaken as agreement is rare and, should there be a misunderstanding, is easily cleared up. Don't be afraid to reflect their true sentiments.

Judgments about Our Values: expert skill level

Before we discuss the most difficult situations for finding empathy, think about these two ideas:

1. Don't blame the messenger
2. Own your own response

1. Don't blame the messenger.

When we don't like the message, we tend to blame our discomfort on how the message was delivered. We condemn the speaker and think, *If only he hadn't shouted*, or *If only she hadn't called me a horrible name*, or *If only he weren't all high and mighty: then I would have listened.* Or we criticize them: *She should have told me in person,* or *He should have discussed it with me first.* On and on, the blaming goes of how the speaker should have acted so that we would react in a way that is consistent with our values.

> Blaming the speaker for our inability to listen is futile, at best.

It is not easy to listen to someone when their message is harsh, but blaming the speaker for our inability to listen is futile, at best. Remember that when people get upset, they *act* upset—we expect them to behave in ways that are not pleasant. Demanding that the speaker talk in a certain manner that is palatable to the listener (so that the listener can do a good job of listening) is definitely not part of the *Tell Me More Gesture*. In fact, it is more like a tell-me-less gesture.

2. Own your own response.

We must, at the very least, decide that we are in charge of our own reactions. Often we demand the speaker to behave in a way that makes it easier for us to listen, and yet we feel entitled to lash out when they do not behave well; this is ironic, at best. So you must own your own response. When you lash out or escalate in any way in response to the speaker's upsetness, it is your own doing. And when you do this, you have moved from listener to speaker. Now there are two speakers and no listeners.

> When we stay with empathy, we allow speakers to touch deeper levels of themselves.
>
> —Marshall B. Rosenberg, *Nonviolent Communication*

Keep in mind the two ideas *Don't blame the messenger* and *Own your own response* as you continue onto this next section of finding empathy for judgments about our inner selves and our values.

When someone doubts or criticizes us for something related to our values, this is extremely hard to listen to. We might feel misunderstood or bullied over qualities that are important to us, such as honesty, kindness, security, or patience. Thinking to yourself, *We disagree and that's OK,* as a way to reserve judgment works wonders here. Then you can move into empathy by thinking, *I'm human too, it's OK.* Here are some illustrations of the choices of judgment, curiosity, and empathy.

SPEAKER: "You never listen to me."
LISTENER:
>   Judgmental: "You should talk!"
>   Curious: "Really?"
>   Empathic: "Oh my, tell me more."

SPEAKER: "You are bossy beyond belief."
LISTENER:
>   Judgmental: "You're a jerk for saying that."
>   Curious: "I'm surprised you say that. When have I
>   been bossy?"
>   Empathic: "That must feel terrible. Tell me more."

SPEAKER: "You've turned into your father."
LISTENER:
>   Judgmental: "Well, at least he had manners."
>   Curious: "Ouch! Why do you say that?"
>   Empathic: "Ooh, I think I've hurt your feelings. Can
>   you tell me more?"

Notice, in the last example, that the curious response lets the person know that their statement hurt and asks them to prove it, while the empathic response does not. The goal is to make the speaker feel listened to, so finding a way to express our own emotional condition is not the best response. Of course, if you are shaken by the statement and cannot muster an empathic response, it is an opportunity for you to utilize the *safety net phrase* "This is really hard, but I'm going to keep trying." And then you can lean forward and say, "Tell me more."

When people are in conflict, their senses are more heightened than in a nonconflict setting. This increased sensitivity can lead to more easily feeling judged, and therefore, your tone of voice as the listener/reflector is

> Behind intimidating messages are merely people appealing to us to meet their needs.
>
> —Marshall B. Rosenberg,
> *Nonviolent Communication*

essential. Look back at the empathic responses above. It would be easy use sarcasm, but then you aren't accomplishing the Gesture. You can convey judgment in your tone of voice even if your words are not judgmental. Being tricky or manipulative by saying words with a snide or condescending voice is definitely not part of the Gesture.

■ ■ ■

When my children, Adam and Rachel, were young, I would tell them that if you are going to apologize for something, you need to do three things: you need to use the person's name, say, "I'm sorry," and say why you are sorry. One day, they were squabbling about something, which resulted in Adam, the younger of the two, hitting Rachel. She was shocked and demanded an apology from him. He looked at her sternly and said, without much inflection, "I'm sorry, Rachel, for hitting you." I noticed his tone of voice, and asked her, "You OK now?" She responded, "No! I want him to say sorry with reverence!"

■ ■ ■

Maybe for good reason, Adam was not ready to apologize, so his apology was not satisfying for Rachel. I credit Rachel's kindergarten teacher with the vocabulary she chose, but the desire for sincerity is real, whether we are children or adults.

Being able to find empathy is developmental, just like learning math or how to ride a bike. We each learn at our own pace. It is easy for some and hard for others, but we can all improve. As adults, we can make the choice to take another's point of view and let go, for the time being, of our own views. When we listen and respond with reverence, with empathy, we welcome a difficult discussion.

> **When we listen and respond with reverence, with empathy, we welcome a difficult discussion.**

Exercise 7.3   Empathy for Judgments about Our Values

[Duration: ten minutes]

For the statements below, write down first how you would normally respond, then write an empathic response. Think about how the conversation might change once you have changed your gesture to one of empathy.

1. SPEAKER: "You never help. You are the laziest person on Earth!"
    LISTENER:
        What I'd like to say: _____
        Empathic response: _____

2. SPEAKER: "How can you call yourself a Christian? You won't give that homeless person money."
    LISTENER:
        What I'd like to say: _____
        Empathic response: _____

3. SPEAKER: "Your idea of art is my idea of a huge waste of money."
    LISTENER:
        What I'd like to say: _____
        Empathic response: _____

4. SPEAKER: "If you had listened to me, you wouldn't be in this mess."
    LISTENER:
        What I'd like to say: _____
        Empathic response: _____

5. SPEAKER: "And you call yourself a good listener. That's a laugh!"
    LISTENER:
        What I'd like to say: _____
        Empathic response: _____

Exercise 7.3   Empathy for Judgments about Our Values

Let's Try It Together

1. SPEAKER: "You never help. You are the laziest person on Earth!"

   LISTENER:

        What I'd like to say: <u>I worked hard all day! Lay off me!</u>

        Empathic response: <u>I never help.</u>

2. SPEAKER: "How can you call yourself a Christian? You won't give that homeless person money."

   LISTENER:

        What I'd like to say: <u>Don't you dare criticize my faith!</u>

        Empathic response: <u>I should be helping that guy.</u>

3. SPEAKER: Your idea of art is my idea of a huge waste of money!

   LISTENER:

        What I'd like to say: <u>What the heck do you care how I spend my money?</u>

        Empathic response: <u>You really hate that painting!</u>

4. SPEAKER: If you had followed my instructions, we wouldn't be in this mess!

   LISTENER:

        What I'd like to say: <u>Oh, right! I guess if I were more like you I'd be so awesome!</u>

        Empathic response: <u>This is all my fault!</u>

5. SPEAKER: And you call yourself a good listener! That's a laugh!

   LISTENER:

        What I'd like to say: <u>You don't ever give me credit for all the times when I did patiently listen.</u>

        Empathic response: <u>I'm a lousy listener!</u>

Know this: If you have hit your limit and are unable to listen further, you should certainly, absolutely, unequivocally take care of yourself. Retriggering trauma is real, and emotional pain is real pain. But it is helpful to understand that these may be your own limitations, not something to be blamed on another person who is upset. Our partners and our families, without trying, know how to push our buttons, so welcoming difficult conversations nearly always feels uncomfortable. I have had to excuse myself to calm down when dealing with my (then teenage) children. These are my limitations. I am human and faulty, and that's OK, but, in the end, the limitations are indeed mine.

> He drew a circle that shut me out,
> Heretic, rebel, a thing to flout.
> But love and I had the wit to win —
> We drew a circle that took him in.
>
> —Edwin Markham,
> American Poet

The Ultimate Test

Finding and expressing empathy while being judged is hard work, and we are now going to ratchet up the difficulty. It is common for conflict experts to set rules about communication tactics that are not allowed. Threatening, name-calling, put-downs, and more are, by their standards, out of bounds. They say, "People must talk respectfully." We, who adopt the Gesture, say, "Then we're missing part of the message." They say, "Foul! Communication killers!" We say, "Tell me more." We appreciate that underneath unpleasant communication tactics are pleas for greater understanding. Check out the following exercise to practice finding empathy when people are at their worst.

Underneath unpleasant communication tactics are pleas for greater understanding.

Exercise 7.4 The Ultimate Test for Empathy

[Duration: fifteen minutes]

For each of the tactics below, write down ideas about ways you can identify with the speaker. (If you're stuck, you can always identify with their human fallibility.) Write an empathic response. (If you're stuck, use a *safety net phrase*.) Notice that you can find empathy for the speaker even when you are confused about *why* they are upset; they will get clearer as you stay with the Gesture.

1. *THREATENING*

   SPEAKER: "If you don't cut it out, I'm out of here!"

   LISTENER:
   Empathic thinking: She is out of choices, at her wit's end.
   Empathic response: Wow, this is a real deal breaker for you!

2. *NAME-CALLING*

   SPEAKER: "Only an idiot would think something like that."

   LISTENER:
   Empathic thinking: _____
   Empathic response: _____

3. *DIAGNOSING*

   SPEAKER: "You only think of yourself. You're a complete narcissist!"

   LISTENER:
   Empathic thinking: _____
   Empathic response: _____

4. *GANGING UP*

   SPEAKER: "You're a control freak. Your whole family thinks so, too."

   LISTENER:
   Empathic thinking: _____
   Empathic response: _____

5. *PUT-DOWNS*

SPEAKER: "You're a waste of time. You'll never make it in this business."

LISTENER:

    Empathic thinking: _____

    Empathic response: _____

6. *SHUTTING YOU DOWN*

SPEAKER: "There's nothing for you to worry about. Just relax!"

LISTENER:

    Empathic thinking: _____

    Empathic response: _____

Exercise 7.4   The Ultimate Test for Empathy

Let's Try it Together

1. *THREATENING*

SPEAKER: "If you don't cut it out, I'm out of here!"

LISTENER:

    Empathy thinking: <u>She is out of choices, at her wit's end, hopeless.</u>

    Empathic response: [leaning forward] <u>Wow, this is a real deal breaker for you!</u>

2. *NAME-CALLING*

SPEAKER: "Only an idiot would think something like that."

LISTENER:

    Empathy thinking: <u>He is upset, panicking, worried.</u>

    Empathic response: <u>So that was pretty stupid.*</u>

3. *DIAGNOSING*

    SPEAKER: "You only think of yourself. You're a complete narcissist!"
    LISTENER:
    Empathy thinking: <u>She is hurt or disappointed; she's really had it; I'm bugging her; she feels left out.</u>
    Empathic response: <u>I only think of myself.</u>*

4. *GANGING UP*

    SPEAKER: "You're a control freak. Your whole family thinks so, too."
    LISTENER:
    Empathy thinking: <u>He is feeling out of control, insecure; he thinks I won't believe him.</u>
    Empathic response: <u>I control everything!</u>

5. *PUT-DOWNS*

    SPEAKER: "You're a waste of time. You'll never make it in this business."
    LISTENER:
    Empathy thinking: <u>She's upset, she is panicking.</u>
    Empathic response: <u>I'm not going to cut it!</u>*

6. *SHUTTING YOU DOWN*

    SPEAKER: For gosh sake, there's nothing to worry about! Just relax!
    LISTENER:
    Empathy thinking: <u>He's anxious, impatient, upset.</u>
    Empathic response: <u>My worrying is really bugging you. Tell me more.</u>

*In many of the responses, it might feel like you are demonstrating agreement if you respond in the suggested ways, but remember that you will find that reflecting in this manner invites more discussion, which is exactly what you want. Notice their emotion is not reflected since they have not stated it.

To be clear, nothing in the Gesture is meant to suggest that you should allow people to mistreat you. If someone is harming you, you have every right to get away. It is important that you take care of yourself, and if the Gesture works for you, it can be added to the many ways of caring for yourself. Finding empathy for someone else should not compromise your values or self-awareness, nor deter you from finding empathy for yourself.

> Finding empathy for someone else should not compromise your values or self-awareness, nor deter you from finding empathy for yourself.

■   ■   ■

My first marriage was to a man who exhibited what I would categorize as several un-husband-like behaviors. While in the marriage, I found it relatively easy to enjoy the positive aspects of our relationship and disregard the negative ones by telling myself that there is a good reason why he turned out the way he did and that his rotten behaviors made perfect sense because his childhood was so crummy. I didn't blame myself, and I didn't blame him either. As you can tell by the phrase "first marriage," we ultimately divorced. I realized years later that I had been finding empathy for him at the expense of having empathy for myself. I was dismissing my own feelings and concentrating on his. This is a survival mechanism where one empathizes with others in order to not feel one's own pain.

■   ■   ■

Staying in or getting out of a relationship has nothing to do with the *Tell Me More Gesture*. The Gesture is intended to enhance any of your relationships, including how you deal with people who treat you badly. When we lower our standards and expectations for our own behavior, the damage is to our own selves. The Gesture empowers you to go through difficult times with grace, integrity, and pride, keeping self-esteem intact.

Moving Forward

Empathy is a wonderful thing. Some people find it easier to achieve than others, but everyone can work at it and improve their skills. If you practice, you will get better. It is similar to learning music: Everyone can train themselves to learn to play an instrument or sing, although some may need more practice than others. Finding empathy and accomplishing the Gesture during times of conflict is a worthwhile endeavor for your own life's enrichment. Practice, practice, practice.

When Pablo Casals (then age 93) was asked why he continued to practice the cello three hours a day, he replied, "I'm beginning to notice some improvement."

—Pablo Casals,
Spanish-born cellist

Journal Entry 7.1

In the exercises in this chapter, what have you noticed that feels different than your normal conflict conversations? What do you notice in yourself, including your emotions, your intellect, and any physical sensations?

_____

_____

_____

_____

_____

_____

_____

_____

_____

_____

_____

_____

_____

_____

_____

Journal Entry 7.2

As you practice finding empathy and making empathic statements when confronted with judgment or disagreement, what are you noticing about yourself that keeps you from being able to accomplish it? What doubts or hurdles do you have?

_____

_____

_____

_____

_____

_____

_____

_____

_____

_____

_____

_____

_____

_____

_____

_____

_____

_____

_____

Please join the Readers' Forum at Janet's website: tellmemoregesture.com. This is a private forum where readers can discuss their successes and struggles of working on the Tell Me More Gesture.

Chapter 8:
GET HOLD OF YOURSELF

Chapter 7 suggested some challenging ideas about finding empathy and welcoming difficult discussions, particularly when people are using language and tactics that are harsh. In some cases, the speaker's behaviors feel hostile and abusive. You have learned that being aware of your motivation to accomplish the Gesture will be your inspiration to lean forward and say, "Tell me more," during difficult, even grueling, conversations.

> You can't pick out the pieces you like and leave the rest. Being part of the whole thing, that's the blessing.
>
> —Natalie Babbit,
> *Tuck Everlasting*

But let's face it: When we are in the middle of a conflict, when we are being treated badly, we react—we get upset. Being mindful of our reactions becomes very difficult. We become focused on ourselves. As we lose our perspective, we cannot see the speaker as a whole person; they become solely the undesirable behavior that they are demonstrating in the moment of conflict. We react badly to them and then fault them for our reactions.

In order to accomplish the Gesture, we must have our own reactions under control. When we can identify and examine our reactions, our triggers, we can stop blaming others for our emotional responses. Personally, I have found that when I can overcome my own discomfort with the way a harsh or blaming message is delivered, I am pleased with my own ability to give empathy in return. Empathy for the other is a balm for oneself.

> Empathy for the other is a balm for oneself.

What Is a Trigger?

A behavioral trigger is any stimulus that affects our reaction, that is, our behavior (Goldsmith and Reiter 2015). In the realm of conflict, a trigger is a negative reaction to a current experience based on a past trauma. Trauma is not always a result of apparent and life-altering experiences such as going to war, being assaulted, surviving a hurricane, or surviving cancer. When we were young we might have been ignored or shamed or belittled—these were all potentially traumatic events that shaped how we react to conflict today.

For the purposes of this book, trauma includes any experience that has been painful and that has had a lasting, harmful effect on one's ability to respond to conflict with empathy. Think of any little reaction you have inside yourself that makes you feel defensive, on edge, a little miffed, resentful, or wary. These inner reactions are caused by triggers from hurts and harms which occurred long ago.

> The past is not dead. In fact, it's not even past.
>
> —William Faulkner, American novelist

We do not all have the same experience of trauma. Here is a story about twin brothers who had very different perceptions of and reactions to the same experience.

■ ■ ■

There once were twin boys who, at age five, like many children, were busy and rambunctious. They had a babysitter who came in once a week to play with the boys and put them to bed while their parents had a night off. Over the years the boys grew into young adults. One of the brothers, Tommy, became a successful businessman and the other, Teddy, had a hard time finding employment that was satisfying, and he struggled to find a meaningful course for his life. Eventually, they were interviewed for an article about twin siblings. When asked why he felt he had struggled so much, Teddy told the interviewer that when he was young, they had had a babysitter who used to shut them in a closet to play hide and seek, and then the babysitter would put spiders under the door. He said that he and his brother had screamed with both delight and fear at the time, but ultimately he was left with an overall sense of anxiety, not about spiders but about people of authority. Teddy reported that his lackluster attitude about his life had come from this event when he was five years old. It affected him in many ways, such as when he would go for a job interview, he would get a stomachache and feel nauseated, similar to how he felt in the closet when he was five. Tommy was interviewed separately, and when asked why he felt he had become a success, he attributed it to the strength and resilience that he had learned as a child when their babysitter had closed them in a closet and put spiders under the door.

■ ■ ■

This is a fine example of similar experiences affecting each of us differently. We do not know what will become a trigger for each of us, but we can understand that triggers are not inherent in any original, undesirable experience. This chapter does not undertake to explain why we do or do not become triggered. It examines what we can do about triggers in order to make way for healthier responses to conflict. That is, how can we overcome our triggers to find empathy for another who might also be triggered?

When our triggers get out of control, we get hijacked—some call it flooded or sidelined. There are many expressions for it, but it means we can no longer help ourselves. When we are triggered, we are reacting on the inside to our old hurts, but we still are able to intellectually understand our inner reactions and have some control over what we do about them. We may have some outer reactions, but we are able to get them under control.

> Resentment is like drinking poison and waiting for the other person to die.
>
> —attributed to various people including: Carrie Fisher, Nelson Mandela, Malachy McCourt, St. Augustine

Once we get hijacked, we are unable to control our outer reactions, and we are emotionally unavailable to another person. Understandably, we are busy taking care of ourselves, protecting ourselves based on our past traumatic experiences. When people get hijacked they are likely to completely lose it, say things they may regret later, or completely shut down. Working on our very first responses to our triggers can help us avoid getting hijacked and, eventually, can even reduce our own initial triggered feelings.

Naming It

When we are triggered, we are upset and headed toward becoming emotionally unavailable. It can be difficult to recognize and to admit to ourselves that we are, in fact, getting overwhelmed with emotions from past trauma. Anytime we cannot access our empathic selves during conflict, we are likely self-absorbed (chapter 1) and triggered. For example, someone yells at me, so I automatically snap back at them. I was triggered by their yelling, and I responded defensively. This is a common response, of course, but it is not the *Tell Me More Gesture*. If I were to have a different impulse, I could stop myself and say, "Tell me more." Of course, there are times when it is appropriate to be self-absorbed. We need to look out for ourselves, advocate for ourselves, and keep ourselves safe. Determining what is, or is not, safe is your decision.

> The enemy to conquer is never a human being.
>
> —Rosamund Zander & Benjamin Zander, *The Art of Possibility*

Admitting that we are self-absorbed during a triggered episode is unpleasant. It can make us feel defective. But we are not defective; we are human. We are supposed to be imperfect and we might as well welcome our imperfections while we are welcoming conflict. Know that our state of being self-absorbed is actually working against us. While we go there to protect ourselves, it also stands in the way of maintaining the human connection that we crave.

When triggered, we might experience physical symptoms such as a flushed face or chills. We might be highly distracted by memory loops of past traumatic events. We might be confused and have a hard time focusing. We might feel righteous about our anger and lashing out. These are all evidence of triggers. After the triggered episode is over, we can think reasonably again, and we may feel sorry about our triggered behavior. If we take the time to examine our discomfort and attribute it to being triggered, sometimes it is enough of a reminder to then change over to our empathic self.

> A righteous or entitled feeling is an indicator of an underlying trigger.

In chapter 1 we discussed how we normally react to people who are upset with us. We escalate, we shut down, we defend, we fix, or we pretend to listen. This may be hard to believe, but all these reactions are a result of being triggered. For example, problem-solving may appear to be a logical reaction to conflict, but it is actually the listener's own discomfort with the conflict that makes them assume that the speaker needs help—so we rush to the rescue. Offering help is not out of line during a normal conversation, although it may be beneficial to listen longer than we normally would.

> Oh yes, the past can hurt. But from the way I see it, you can either run from it, or learn from it.
>
> —Rafiki,
> *The Lion King*

Even when we are quiet, when we appear to be listening, we are likely running scenarios in our heads about how we can help, how we can shut them up, or how we can get away. All of these impulses are because of our own triggers. We have been knocked off our game and are not utilizing our strengths, but dealing from weakness, difficulty, or damage—the result of our own triggers.

Take a look at the following chart, which shows common underlying triggers that would explain our negative conflict reactions. Notice that any of the triggers in the right-hand column could produce any of the reactions in the left column; this is different for everyone.

Conflict Reactions	Common Underlying Triggers
Escalating/lashing out	Chaos, need for control
Shutting down/avoiding	Fear
Defending	Feeling disrespected
Fixing/problem-solving	Feeling shame, embarrassment
Pretending to listen	Feeling undervalued, unappreciated, dismissed
	Injustice, lack of fairness
	Lack of security
	Loneliness, loss
	Not getting heard, no voice

Let's think about lashing out, in particular. You cannot rationalize lashing out or feeling anger simply because you disagree vehemently. People commonly disagree without lashing out in anger. Even feeling the anger (without lashing out) is a triggered response. There is no shame in having these responses. They are perfectly understandable and very human, however, they are not always productive responses and can keep you from truly taking care of yourself.

> Anger is valuable, especially in a family situation, because it is a raw and fresh expression of one's heart's desire – the genuine need. Learning to listen to each other's anger allows us to hear the heart's desire.
>
> —Jeanne Elium & Don Elium, *Raising a Family*

This is the irony: While anger can be useful—it demonstrates that someone is passionate about a topic or has reached their limit, and it may motivate one to make necessary change—it is still a triggered response. We expect to get triggered at times—it is human—but we are trying to name it for what it is, a triggered response, which then allows us to make a conscious decision about whether it is or is not valuable at that moment.

Use the following exercise to determine the triggers that might be underlying your own negative conflict reactions. Notice that *Let's Try It Together* appears before the exercise as an example.

When I did this exercise, this is what I discovered about myself:

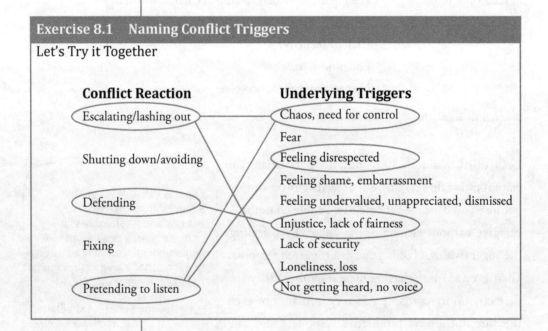

Exercise 8.1   Naming Conflict Triggers

Let's Try it Together

Conflict Reaction	Underlying Triggers
Escalating/lashing out	Chaos, need for control
	Fear
Shutting down/avoiding	Feeling disrespected
	Feeling shame, embarrassment
Defending	Feeling undervalued, unappreciated, dismissed
	Injustice, lack of fairness
Fixing	Lack of security
	Loneliness, loss
Pretending to listen	Not getting heard, no voice

Exercise 8.1   Naming Conflict Triggers

[Duration: five minutes]

1. In the left-hand column of chart below, circle any of the conflict reactions that you recognize in yourself. (It is possible you will circle all of the options.)

2. In the right-hand column, read the list to see if you recognize in yourself any of the underlying triggered feelings. Feel free to add to the list. Circle any of them that are true for you.

3. Draw a line from each of the behaviors (on the left) to each of the triggers (on the right) where there seems to be a connection. There may be two (or more) triggers for a behavior and two (or more) behaviors for a trigger.

4. Use Journal Entry 8.1 at the end of this chapter to write about your findings in this exercise.

Conflict Reaction	Underlying Triggers
Escalating/lashing out	Chaos, need for control
	Fear
Shutting down/avoiding	Feeling disrespected
	Feeling shame, embarrassment
Defending	Feeling undervalued, unappreciated, dismissed
	Injustice, lack of fairness
Fixing	Lack of security
	Loneliness, loss
Pretending to listen	Not getting heard, no voice
	_____
	_____

Trigger Igniters

It is important to recognize that there are contributing factors in peoples' lives that reduce their resiliency and their ability to cope well with conflict. I call these *trigger igniters*. Triggers appear at some moments and not others because of everyday occurrences, such as being tired, hungry, or otherwise stressed. These leave us feeling weaker and less patient than our normal selves. We are more likely to have a triggered response when any one of them is present. Following is a list of trigger igniters. Check the box next to any that might be true for you, and add to the list any igniters you think of that are not listed here.

Trigger Igniters

- ☐ Hunger, low blood sugar—Are you one who gets *hangry*?
- ☐ Time pressure—Running out of time, running late
- ☐ Lack of sleep—Tired, cranky
- ☐ Drained—Physically exhausted
- ☐ Stress—Unemployment, overwork, poverty, other conflicts, sickness, deaths, funerals, etc.
- ☐ Eustress—Weddings, graduations, births, birthdays, holidays, etc.
- ☐ Influence of alcohol and other drugs
- ☐ _____
- ☐ _____

Our underlying triggers are always inside of us. Igniters serve to fan the flame of any underlying trigger that is being challenged during conflict. We all commonly experience many, if not all, of the above conditions. We cannot avoid them, but we can reduce their effect on us by becoming conscious of them. We then can take responsibility for the way they affect our ability to productively deal with conflict. In other words:

$$\text{Underlying Triggers} + \text{Igniters} + \text{Disagreement/Difficulty} = \text{Conflict Reaction/Triggered Behavior}$$

Notice that in the above formula for a conflict reaction, there is no mention of the conflict on the left side of the equation. The conflict is not inherent; it does not exist without your internal reaction and external response to the difficulty. You can interrupt the progress of the equation toward conflict reaction (triggered behaviors) by becoming aware of the separate elements and changing your conflict reaction.

Changing Your Conflict Reaction

Following are ideas for overcoming the triggered behaviors that keep us from remaining connected to others (and to ourselves) so that we can become our best, empathic selves during conflict. These are things you can do in the moment of conflict to help yourself move away from triggered behavior and stay with the Gesture.

1.   Own your contribution
2.   Know that you only control yourself
3.   Decide who you want to be
4.   Make a new plan
5.   Have fortitude

1.   Own your contribution

> There are valid reasons from our past for why we each respond to conflict the way we do, but clinging to the reasons does not serve us well in the present.

There are valid reasons from our past for why we each respond to conflict the way we do, but clinging to the reasons does not serve us well in the present. In order to get through any conflict, you must understand that you are not the victim. You are in this situation for many reasons, you had a hand in getting there, and owning your part is important to changing your reactions.

It takes plenty of personal awareness to be able to own our contribution. Zander and Zander's (2002) concept of "being the board" is a useful notion here. We decide to accept this idea: "[I] rename [myself] as the board on which the whole game is being played," and indeed, "I am the framework for everything that happens in my life" (pages 141 & 142). That is, I take responsibility for every part of every single thing in which I am involved. I understand that I have made decisions that have contributed to my circumstances. Zander and Zander's definition of grace sums this up eloquently. "Grace comes from owning the risks we take in a world by and large immune to our control" (page 143).

Giving recognition until the distressed, emotional speaker is all-the-way done while being triggered is extremely challenging. This is not how normal conflict conversations happen. We are usually eager for the upset speaker to stop talking so that we can begin talking, or so that we can go away. Accepting that there are inherent risks by merely being out in the world will help you to not feel like a victim. You can think to yourself, *I have some causal effect for how I got to this place, and I decided to do the Tell Me More Gesture.* Remembering that learning the Gesture is your choice, not something that you are required to do, is empowering and reassuring.

> Grace comes from owning the risks we take in a world by and large immune to our control.
>
> —Rosamund Zander & Benjamin Zander, *The Art of Possibility*

This notion can be a big leap to take when you are in the middle of a conflict, and you are being blamed or belittled. So remember this: The person who is doing the raging or blaming is merely being who they are. Think to yourself, *They are upset. They have a certain set of beliefs, which do not match mine. Their stating an opinion in a way that is not very appealing does not make me their victim. We disagree and that's OK.* The following Buddhist parable is a perfect example of the notion that you are not a victim when in conflict. This story has been told a variety of ways—here is an adaptation of the one told by Goldsmith and Reiter (2015):

■ ■ ■

A farmer was covered with sweat as he paddled his boat up the river. He was going upstream to deliver his produce to the village, trying to make the round trip before dark. As he looked ahead he spied another vessel, heading rapidly downstream toward his boat. He rowed frantically to get out of the way, but it didn't seem to help. He shouted, "Change direction! You are going to hit me!" but to no avail. The vessel hit his boat with a violent thud. He cried out, "You idiot! How could you manage to hit my boat in the middle of this wide river?" As he glared into the boat, seeking out the individual responsible for the accident, he realized no one was there. He had been screaming at an empty boat that had broken free of its moorings and was floating downstream with the current.

■   ■   ■

The moral of this story is: It is always an empty boat. The parent who never acknowledged you, the driver who suddenly cut you off, the boss who berated you—they are all empty boats. They were acting based on their own unexamined or unresolved psychological suffering, their triggers. It had nothing to do with you.

Notice that we are not angry at an empty boat. We are only angry if there is someone at its helm. In conflict, the boat is always empty. When there is no one in the boat, we are forced to look at the only person on hand: our self. We can think to ourselves, *I was the one rowing upriver. I did not have enough control over my own boat. I was rushing and didn't leave enough time. I take a chance that something could happen every time I enter the river. The river is inherently dangerous.*

> Pain that is not transformed is transferred.
>
> —Richard Rohr, Franciscan priest

Admitting your own contribution sounds painful, but is surprisingly liberating. When we feel victimized by others, we overlook the control we do have. When we are in the middle of conflict, we often feel victimized by the other person, which gives way to our own triggered behaviors. When this happens to you, try this quick exercise in your head: Make a list with two columns. "Their Fault" is the header on the left, and "My Fault" is on the right. Imagine that the left-hand "Their Fault" column is chock full with panicked scribbling. You have already filled out that column twenty times over. Now look at the right-hand "My Fault" column. It is completely empty. Fill out that right-hand column by saying to yourself, *What did I do to contribute to my being in this conflict situation right now?* The following exercise is practice for accomplishing this thought process:

Exercise 8.2   My Conflict Contribution

[Duration: five minutes]

Think of a specific person with whom you might have an argument. Imagine you are having a difficult discussion in which they are very upset with you. Write down all of the things that you can own about your own contribution to the conflict.

Their Fault	My Fault
Blah blah blah blah	_____
Blah blah blah blah	_____
Blah blah blah blah	_____
Blah blah blah blah	_____
Blah blah blah blah	_____
Blah blah blah blah	_____

Exercise 8.2   My Conflict Contribution

Let's Try It Together

Their Fault	My Fault
Blah blah blah blah	I shut them down.
Blah blah blah blah	I reacted badly.
Blah blah blah blah	I could have listened more.
Blah blah blah blah	I never showed my appreciation.
Blah blah blah blah	I got defensive.
Blah blah blah blah	I'm overtired.
Blah blah blah blah	I committed to this relationship.

2. Know that you only control yourself

No matter how well you say things, how kindly you broach a topic, how much awesome listening you do, you cannot force someone to respond in a way that you desire. You can't prevent them from getting upset, and you can't control how they handle their upsetness.

> Like failure, chaos contains information that can lead to knowledge – even wisdom.
>
> —Toni Morrison, American novelist

Chaos is a common precursor for trying to control others. This is an attempt to feel in control ourselves. When we perceive, rightly or otherwise, that things are spiraling out of control, we lose confidence in the process. Conflict is messy. It does not go in a straight line. We have to open our minds to listening to information and witnessing behaviors that are confusing and offensive, and that could ignite our underlying triggers.

■　■　■

Jonathan was a calm, soft-spoken computer programmer who worked cooperatively with two other programmers. They would talk aloud with each other to generate ideas and work out solutions. Kim, one of the other programmers, would get extremely animated during these discussions—some might call it agitated—sometimes directing her distress at the other programmers. She would stand up and pace, flailing her arms while trying to get her point across. I remember Jonathan leaning forward with his arms resting on his desk, raising up his chin, squinting his eyes thoughtfully, and just listening while Kim got around to figuring out what she was trying to say. He told me one time that he admired her creative thinking, and it was always worth it if he could wade through the process.

■　■　■

Jonathan's behavior was communicating to Kim, "Tell me more," even though he was struggling to understand where she was headed. Without any words, his receptiveness exuded the Gesture.

When we search for control we say things like, "I demand you speak to me with respect!" or "You go calm down and then maybe I'll listen!" Mediators make rules such as "no interrupting," "must use respectful language," etc. If people could do that, they probably wouldn't need help. Ensuring that people feel comfortable to say what they need to say, and helping the other party feel comfortable to not judge the other participant, is part of the work mediators should be

> We can be so busy criticizing the way the speaker is behaving that we miss the message.

> There is only one rule for
> being a good talker – learn
> to listen.
>
> – Christopher Morley,
> American journalist

doing. This is the same work we can do as we listen to someone during conflict. We can be so busy criticizing the way they are behaving that we miss the message.

Noticing this impulse in yourself during conflict can be a cue for you to try something new. When you are tempted to ask someone to restate something or to tell them that their logic is ridiculous, instead try to *not* control them. Try opening up your mind and changing your listening. Think about listening as if you are hearing a foreign language that you do not understand very well, so you must listen to the whole meaning instead of picking words apart. Now, lean forward, and say, "Tell me more."

3.   Decide who you want to be

When we are triggered, we are dealing from our damaged selves. We might feel criticized, jealous, unheard, or a multitude of other emotions. If we have decided ahead of time who we want to be, we can access that information as we are beginning to feel triggered.

■ ■ ■

Many years ago, when my first husband and I were divorcing, we decided that the best thing (for a while) for our family would be a bird's nest arrangement. This means that the children remain at home and the parents are the ones who come and go. As a result, we were forced to deal with each other directly and to continue to work together to maintain the home. One day I came home to a clean kitchen—lovely, and not out of the ordinary—but when I opened the dishwasher it was chock full of dishes and pans with dried-on food. Our dishwasher would never get that stuff clean.

I felt my face get hot, remembering all of the other things that I didn't like about how *he* treated me. I closed up the dishwasher figuring I would leave it there for the next time he would be home. *He can deal with it!* Pause. I then thought to myself, *OK, Janet, how did you say you want to be in this divorce? Are you really going to let this derail you?* So I reopened the dishwasher, took out the filthy dishes, and rinsed them well in the sink. Within fifteen minutes the dishwasher was reloaded, closed up, turned on—and then, a rush of pride. Not giving in to the trigger was exhilarating.

■   ■   ■

I had decided the type of person I wanted to be during my divorce. I wanted to be nonreactive and calm, neither of which came naturally to me. I wanted my children to experience us still appreciating each other. I didn't always do a perfect job of this, but I tried really hard, and mostly I pulled it off. The more I practiced, the more I became the person I wanted to be.

Understanding why you have chosen to adopt the *Tell Me More Gesture* is part of deciding who you want to be. This will help you manage your triggers, because you are urging your highest self to be present during a conflict. This is a good time to revisit your conflict mantra card that you made in chapter 3. Why did you decide to do the Gesture? Do you still feel the same way? Journal Exercise 8.2 at the end of this chapter will help you flesh out some of your feelings.

> In all chaos there is a cosmos, in all disorder a secret order.
>
> —Carl Jung,
> Swiss Psychiatrist

4. Make a new plan

I remember being told by a therapist, "If you can see your triggered symptoms, then you do not have to become the trigger." If you can recognize your own triggered symptoms, then you can change your response. This is difficult to accomplish, because you have to stop yourself just as you are revving up for your standard, ingrained response on your way to being hijacked. But then it's too late. You must do this self-reflection in advance and have a plan in mind for the next time it occurs. What are your physical and emotional symptoms? Once you can recognize the symptoms, you are more equipped to make a change.

■ ■ ■

When my children were in high school, I found myself easily triggered—I would raise my voice and lash out. It would happen most often when I was under time pressure to leave the house or when my teenager had homework or a project due the very next day. Generally I would feel unappreciated, disrespected, and a need to get matters under control (see some of the common underlying triggers on page 173). Not only is time pressure a trigger igniter (page 176) for me, but also I was often sleep deprived. When all of this coalesced, I became extremely impatient and panicked, and I would feel like a cylindrical, red-and-black metal helmet would come down over my head and face. I learned that this is a warning sign for me—I am triggered when this is happening. With practice, I could break my own pattern and stop myself from lashing out. My new behavior would be to calm myself by telling myself that how I treat people is more important than time pressure. If I could not calm down quickly, I would take a break until I could change my attitude and my behavior.

■ ■ ■

Here are some common indicators of being triggered:

Stomach pain	Impatience
Dry mouth	Nausea
Headache	Sweating
Racing heartbeat	Adrenaline rush
Tightness in chest	Confusion
Ringing in ears	Inability to articulate
Tunnel vision, myopia	Panic
Shallow breathing	Feelings of entitlement

In my story on the previous page, I noted my conflict behavior of lashing out along with my trigger igniters, time pressure and fatigue. The following exercise will help you discover your own symptoms when you are on the way to being triggered. Based on this story, here is what I discovered about myself, as an example.

Exercise 8.3   Naming Triggered Symptoms

Let's Try It Together

Conflict Reaction: Lashing out

Underlying Trigger: Lack of control

Trigger Igniter(s):   Time pressure, stress, fatigue

Characteristics and indicators that preceded my conflict reaction:

Reddish-black mask comes down over my head

Extremely impatient

Feelings of entitlement

Exercise 8.3   Naming Triggered Symptoms

[Duration: 10 minutes for each conflict reaction]

1. Choose one of your circled conflict reactions (page 174). Write it here:

    _____

2. Write down the underlying trigger(s) for that conflict reaction (page 174):

    _____

3. Write down your common igniters (page 176):

    _____

4. Imagine a specific situation where your conflict reaction occurred. Take a few minutes to consider your own physical and emotional reactions as you were getting triggered. What were your physical and emotional feelings?

5. Articulate these feelings aloud to yourself, as if you are describing the symptoms to someone else. Do you notice that you are gesturing to help convey the feeling?

6. Write down the symptoms/characteristics of your physical and emotional feelings:

    _____

    _____

    _____

    _____

    _____

    _____

    _____

    _____

Taking the time to accomplish exercise 8.3 for *each* of your conflict reactions (that you circled in exercise 8.1) will help you take responsibility and not blame someone for your behavior. Note: Admitting that defending and fixing are triggered responses to conflict can be a hurdle. Remember that while they might be appropriate responses during a normal conversation, they are not appropriate in the height of a conflict. Exercise 8.3 will help you examine this.

Once you have identified your specific triggered characteristics and indicators, you can make a plan to change the pattern of how you respond. Good news: The more you work to recognize these triggered responses, the less often you will feel triggered. You can actually reduce your triggered-ness by merely recognizing your triggered state.

Now that you can recognize your triggered characteristics and indicators, you need to find a way to change your response from a negative conflict reaction to the *Tell Me More Gesture*. In times of conflict, we want to stop acting impulsively and start acting intentionally, mindfully, in a way that keeps our relationships and our integrity intact. When we are feeling triggered, we want to stop those triggered impulses, lean forward, and say, "Tell me more." Here are some ideas for how to change your conflict reactions:

> A senior monk and a junior monk were traveling together. They came to a river with a strong current. As the monks were preparing to cross the river, they saw a woman also attempting to cross. The woman asked if they could help her to cross to the other side, however the monks had taken vows not to touch a woman.
>
> Then, without a word, the older monk picked up the woman, carried her across the river, placed her gently on the other side, and carried on his journey. The junior monk was shaken.
>
> Hours had passed when finally the junior monk blurted out, "As monks, we are not permitted to touch a woman, how could you then carry that woman on your shoulders?"
>
> The older monk replied, "Brother, I left the woman hours ago, but I see you are still carrying her."
>
> —Buddhist parable

(1) **Notice your triggered symptoms** and think, *Oh, hello! I recognize you. I know you have come to protect me, but this isn't a good time for you to be here. Please wait outside for now*. Depending on the severity of the trigger, acknowledging the presence of the trigger may be enough help for you to move forward. You can now say, "Tell me more."

(2) **Change your breathing** to help eliminate the triggered feelings. Do a mini-meditation such as this:

> Breathe in through your nose.
> Hold it for just a moment. Then breathe out through your nose.
> Breathe in again, noticing the physical sensation on your nostrils.
> Now breathe out, notice that the sensation is different.
> Breathe in again, hold it briefly, and breathe out while continuing to notice the different sensations of inhaling and exhaling.
> Do this at least three more times.

When you use a brief meditation like this, you will be surprised at the positive effect on your emotions and your ability to stay focused on the speaker. You *can* accomplish this while listening. You may now be able to lean forward and say, "Tell me more."

If you are unable to shake your triggered feelings, (3) **make a quick note** of what made you feel that way. Writing it down can help you let go of it, at least for the moment. Now you can get back to responding to the conflict with empathic listening.

If you try these first three things and are unable to shake the triggered feelings, you may need to **(4) take a break**. Understand that your capacity to communicate in this triggered moment is diminished, so if you need to take a break, try to say so without blame. For example, "I'm too upset to continue. I need to take a break." You should also estimate how much time you might need before you can give it another try. For example, "I'd be willing to try again in twenty minutes." When you return, you can begin the conversation by leaning forward and saying, "OK, I'm ready to try again. Please tell me more." Know that using a break in order to shut down the speaker is not part of the Gesture. Your intention must to be to give yourself a break, not to exert control over the other person.

> You do not have to be good. You do not have to walk on your knees for a hundred miles through the desert, repenting. You only have to let the soft animal of your body love what it loves.
>
> —Mary Oliver, American poet

Changing your triggered behavior patterns is not easy work, but remember this: You can stop the triggered reactions and begin the Gesture at any time. First comes the impulse and you remember, *Oh! I wanted to say, "Tell me more!"* Then you just begin it by saying something like, "Sorry, hang on! I want to do this differently. Please tell me more." The impulse itself will be a comfort to you. You will think, *Right! I can do the Gesture instead of acting triggered. Now I can begin to feel good about my part in this.*

5. Have fortitude. (or) **It's only easy when it's easy.**

Accomplishing the first four items on the list is relatively simple to do when you are not in the middle of a conflict. It is easy to live to our values when all

> If you only walk on sunny days you'll never reach your destination.
>
> —Paulo Coelho, Brazilian lyricist and novelist

> **When matters get difficult, living to our values is a challenge, and this is when it counts most.**

is going well. Being kind, patient, or forgiving in our everyday, nonconflict interactions is commendable, but when matters get difficult, living to our values is a challenge, and this is when it counts most.

Finding the fortitude to live to our values in times of difficulty is challenging; that is why it is called difficulty! There is no way around this. We must persevere: Keep trying, appreciate progress, forgive failures, and try again. Like learning a musical instrument, a foreign language, yoga, meditation, or a martial art, the work is ongoing. There are always more and new ways to apply our new understandings. Accomplishing the *Tell Me More Gesture* is not a place you arrive—it is a practice.

Resources for Healing

This chapter is not intended to serve as a replacement for therapeutic work on one's traumas and triggers. This chapter provides help for moving through conflict without triggered reactions, yet our unexamined wounds can remain and continue to trouble us and keep us from being the person we want to be. Dealing with our triggers in the ways suggested above may provide some healing, as the process itself can be therapeutic, but healing may require other assistance.

Living with intention means that we aspire to be aware of our damage or our hurdles and to free ourselves from their negative effects. Everyone has traumatic memories, although the degree of trauma and negative effect on one's life varies greatly. And everyone has developed coping mechanisms to protect themselves from real or perceived harms. These coping mechanisms can be negative ones—the ones that produce triggered, out-of-control reactions.

Traumas run the gamut from the part-of-growing-up-and-being-human-type of traumas to more severe traumas such as combat service; severe neglect; emotional, physical, or sexual abuse; and physical and sexual assault. The circumstances of a traumatic event commonly include abuse of power and betrayal of trust, feelings of being trapped, helplessness, pain, confusion, or loss. This definition of trauma is quite broad and purposefully does not allow people to determine what is traumatic for others. That evaluation is up to each individual (Vermilyea 2013).

There are many sources of help for trauma survivors who want to transform their lives and minimize the effects of and find meaning from their traumatic experience. In The Little Book of Trauma Healing (2005), Yoder details a journey of healing that includes:

1. Finding safety, breaking free
2. Mourning, grieving
3. Accepting the reality of the loss
4. Reflecting, understanding root causes, acknowledging the enemy's story, facing own shortcomings
5. Committing to take risks
6. Tolerance, coexistence
7. Engaging the offender (or society)
8. Choosing to forgive
9. Acknowledging responsibility, restitution, creative justice
10. Negotiating solutions

11. Integrating trauma into new self/group identity

12. Possibility of reconciliation

Notice that regardless of the severity of one's trauma, these are emotionally nourishing ideas. There is valuable wisdom to be gleaned when one looks more deeply into each concept in this "little" book.

Doing personal work can feel uncomfortable and risky. In *Growing Beyond Survival* (2013), Vermilyea suggests that awareness can be a two-edged sword. It is certainly the cure for avoidance, yet it puts one in touch with thoughts and feelings that can be extremely distressing. It is work that requires patience, fortitude, and self-compassion.

> Traumatic events and times have the potential to awaken the best of the human spirit.
>
> —Carolyn Yoder,
> *The Little Book of Trauma Healing*

If our discussion of triggers and trauma is leading you to deepen your awareness or search out help, there are many therapeutic approaches available. Begin with something that rings true for you. Following is a (non-exhaustive) list of therapies with brief descriptions to serve as a resource for you to investigate further, as you desire or deem appropriate.

Styles of therapies

Behavior therapy is focused on helping one to understand how changing their behavior can lead to changes in how they are feeling. The goal is usually focused on increasing the person's engagement in positive or socially reinforcing activities. Behavior therapy is a structured approach that carefully measures what the person is doing and then seeks to increase chances for positive experience (Psych Central 2016).

Cognitive behavioral therapy (CBT) is based on the principle that thoughts (cognitions) cause our feelings and behaviors. Therefore, correcting one's problematic underlying assumptions and then teaching rational self-counseling skills is at the core of this technique (National Association of Cognitive-Behavioral Therapists n.d.).

Eye movement desensitization and reprocessing (EMDR) therapy concentrates on determining what is useful to you from an experience which will be learned and stored with appropriate emotions in your brain, and will be able to guide you in positive ways in the future. The inappropriate emotions, beliefs, and body sensations will be discarded (EMDRIA n.d.).

Exposure therapy involves slowly confronting the objects or situations that provoke one's anxiety. As one begins to face fears, anxiety will naturally decrease during the "exposure." After multiple exposures, the object or situation will evoke less and less anxiety each time, and patients then usually move up to more difficult or anxiety-producing objects or situations (EBBP.org n.d.).

Group therapy is a shared therapeutic experience that involves the presence of a trained professional and others who are working through similar issues. This collaborative form of healing focuses on particular concerns shared by group members or on interpersonal relationships (GoodTherapy. org n.d.).

Hypnotherapy is a skilled verbal communication used during hypnosis, which helps direct a client's imagination in such a way as to bring about intended alterations in sensations, perceptions, feelings, thoughts, and behavior. In a typical session, the hypnotherapist will ask the client questions about previous medical history, general health, and lifestyle. The hypnotherapist and client will decide together on the changes or goals that are desired (National Hypnotherapy Society n.d.).

Pharmacotherapy, commonly referred to as **drug therapy**, is when medication is prescribed to help correct a disorder by the delivery of drugs. Drugs interact with receptors or enzymes in cells to promote healthy functioning and reduce or cure illness. It is usually recommended that drug therapy be used in concert with other therapy or therapies (CRC Health Group. n.d.).

Positive psychotherapy focuses on growth as opposed to diagnosis. Seligman (2011) concludes that there is a self-fulfilling nature to diagnosis which can then catasrophize one's experiences. Positive psychotherapy works toward creating well-being through discovering and cultivating one's signature strengths by asking *what is right with you* instead of *what is wrong with you (*Seligman 2011).

Psychodynamic therapy focuses on the psychological roots of emotional suffering. Its hallmarks are self-reflection and self-examination, and the use of the relationship between therapist and patient as a window into problematic relationship patterns in the patient's life. Its goal is not only to alleviate the most obvious symptoms but to help people lead healthier lives (Shedler 2010).

Moving Forward

In chapter 8 we have taken a frank look at triggers. We examined them in order to recognize them in ourselves, a first step to overcoming them. We discussed that when we are not able to be empathic during a difficult conversation (when we respond by lashing out, being defensive, going into fix-it mode, avoiding the conversation, or pretending to listen), this is evidence of being triggered. We then looked at how to help ourselves change our conflict responses from triggered to empathic. We must own our contribution, understand deeply that we only control ourselves, decide who we want to be, make a plan to behave differently, and have fortitude.

Examining oneself is hard work and can be downright unpleasant. The bad news is that not being willing to look at one's triggers is a symptom of the depth of one's difficulties. That is, the more you are compelled to avoid investigating your triggers, the more work there may be to accomplish. The good news is that while the work is very difficult, it will yield great benefits—for your own satisfaction and for the improvement of your relationships.

Finding the wherewithal to use the *Tell Me More Gesture* requires one to be brutally honest with oneself, but it is also essential to be self-accepting and compassionate about one's difficulties. Before you move on to chapter 9, please take fifteen to twenty minutes to complete the journal questions for this chapter.

> The ultimate measure of a man is not where he stands in moments of comfort and convenience, but where he stands at times of challenge and controversy.
>
> —Rev. Martin Luther King, Jr, Baptist minister and civil rights leader.

Journal Entry 8.1

In exercise 8.1 (page 175), you were asked to note your conflict reactions and connect them to their underlying triggers. You also learned about igniters and their role in increasing the likelihood of negative conflict behaviors. Spend some time reflecting on and writing about these specific connections and how they play out in different relationships in your life.

_____

_____

_____

_____

_____

_____

_____

_____

_____

_____

_____

_____

_____

_____

_____

_____

_____

Journal Entry 8.2

Originally in chapter 3, and now here in chapter 8, you have been encouraged to be aware of why you want to adopt the *Tell Me More Gesture*. Reflect on your learning journey up to this point. Do you have new insights about how the Gesture benefits you? Do you have new ideas about why you want to accomplish the Gesture? In what areas of your life might this be useful?

_____

_____

_____

_____

_____

_____

_____

_____

_____

_____

_____

_____

_____

_____

_____

_____

_____

_____

_____

Please join the Readers' Forum at Janet's website: tellmemoregesture.com. This is a private forum where readers can discuss their successes and struggles of working on the Tell Me More Gesture.

Chapter 9:
PUTTING IT ALL TOGETHER

Finding the wherewithal to use the *Tell Me More Gesture* requires one to be self-reflective, but it is also essential to be self-accepting and compassionate about our own human frailties. This includes accepting that we are human, that we are highly imperfect, and that making change is difficult.

> Listening is an attitude of the heart, a genuine desire to be with another which both attracts and heals.
>
> —L.J. Isham

Up to this point we have examined the Gesture in small bits: *safety net phrases*, *quick phrase reflections*, *short list reflections*, opening up the conversation, reserving judgment, finding empathy, getting hold of ourselves while triggered, and more. This list of do's and don'ts can feel daunting when all you want to do is get through the conflict.

In reality, once you begin the Gesture by simply leaning forward and saying, "Tell me more," the conversation will take on a natural flow that allows you to be in the moment with the speaker, without thinking about each specific skill. Once you start it, the process begins, and you will see many opportunities to show empathy, as well as a few temptations to respond in old, unwanted ways. You may want to focus on one or two specific skills at a time.

Let's look at how a conversation might develop to help illustrate the Gesture as a whole. Following is a neighbor conflict scenario that demonstrates how the Gesture plays out. Realistically, it takes a few moments for one of the neighbors to begin the Gesture. Read it once disregarding the explanatory notes underneath each line in order to get a feel for the rhythm of the Gesture, then go back and read it a second time and include the notes.

◉ ◉ ◉

Neighbor Conflict

June: [leaning over the backyard fence] "You know you've got to shut up that dog of yours! I've had it!"

Fay: [sitting in her lawn chair with her dog asleep] "Oh c'mon lady! My dog is sweet!"

> *Fay does not immediately think to begin the Gesture. She responds defensively.*

June: "See! You're a bitch! I can't take it anymore!"

> *June gets more upset, demonstrating her feeling weak and self-absorbed.*

Fay: "WHAT?"

> *Fay is still shocked, but not lashing out in return.*

June: "Seriously, you've gotten on my last nerve! I'm going to call the police!"

Fay: [turns listener] "Wait, wait! What? Me?"

June: "Yes, you! You're a jerk!"

Notice that June has already reduced her name calling from "bitch" to "jerk" once Fay begins to listen.

Fay: "I'm a jerk!" [pause]

Fay consciously begins the Gesture here. She resolves to find empathy for June.

June: "I can't take it anymore!"

June is focusing on her own feelings rather than continuing to call Fay names.

Fay: [getting up and moving closer to June] "You've had it!"

Similar to leaning forward, Fay moves toward June, as a signal that she is truly engaged. Fay has no idea what is wrong but is not asking specific questions. She finds empathy for June's upset feeling regardless of the reason.

June: "Yes, I've had it! Are you kidding me?"

Fay: "It's gotten really bad!"

June: "Not just bad, horrendous!"

Even though Fay missed the mark on how bad it is for June, it gives June the opportunity to say more and to get clear on her feelings.

Fay: "Really terrible!" [pause] "Tell me more."

Fay pauses to see if June is going to continue. When June does not, Fay lets her know she would like to understand better.

June: "That dog of yours barks incessantly!"

This is the first piece of real information from June—a signal that she is a bit calmer.

Fay: "My dog is obnoxious."

Fay has no idea what June is talking about but decides to just believe June.

June: "Yes! That barking is crazy-making!"

Fay: "It's making you crazy!" [pauses to see if there is more]

Fay does not quiz June about how often the dog barks, how long the episodes last, etc. Fay just believes her.

Fay: "And I heard you say that not only my dog is obnoxious, but I'm a jerk, too."

Fay is willing to bring up the other tough stuff that was said. This is a fantastic example of putting your head in the lion's mouth.

June: "Well, 'jerk' might be strong."

Fay: "So, I might bug you, but this is more about my dog."

June: "No, you don't bug me. You're mostly a good neighbor, but your dog's yapping is unbearable."

June is getting clear that it really isn't about Fay. It's about the dog.

Fay: "What the heck are you talking about? We've been sitting here quietly minding our own business! This is too much!"

Suddenly Fay is triggered. She has been an awesome neighbor to June and has done many kind deeds for her. In fact, Fay has spent a lot of time clearing June's sidewalk in the winter because June is not able to do it. Fay feels really burdened that June is griping.

June: "See! There you go! You attack me when I'm the one being harmed!"

Fay: "OK, I'm sorry. Please continue. I want to hear more about what's going on for you. Please tell me more."

> *Notice that Fay is the one apologizing even though June was accusing and name-calling. The speaker might eventually apologize for those behaviors, but requiring an apology from the speaker is not part of the Gesture. Fay has now returned to doing the Gesture.*

June: [warily] "OK, well, Lacy has been barking at night while you're at work. It has been going on for months. She has one of those yappy voices that drive me crazy, and it's incessant."

> *June does get back to her complaints. Fay's outburst doesn't completely blow the conversation because ultimately what June wants is to be heard.*

Fay: "OK, hang on. So, Lacy has been constantly barking while I'm gone. And her yappy voice makes it worse. And it's been going on for months."

> *Fay begins using short list reflections now that June is talking in paragraphs and giving real information. Fay knows that it hasn't been going on for months because she has had this night job for only five weeks, but she does not say this. She stays in the Gesture. She knows what it's like to exaggerate to make your point or that it might feel like it's been many months, so Fay finds empathy for June and continues.*

June: "Yes, after you leave she starts barking. It stops for periods of maybe twenty minutes but then it starts up again. Off and on constantly until you get home."

Fay never asks for the specifics, and June is now giving them to her without ever being quizzed.

Fay: "She might stop for a bit but then it starts up again."

June: Yes. She barks and barks. Off and on constantly until you get home."

June repeats herself.

Fay: "Off and on, constantly."

Fay doesn't mention that June is repeating herself. Fay is mindful to state the portion that was repeated to reassure June that she is getting heard.

June: "Yes. Exactly. I haven't slept, Fay. My sleep has been completely disrupted. I don't even feel like myself anymore. I haven't said anything because you have done so many nice things for me. You're a great neighbor. And I don't want to complain. But now I feel like a grouchy, bitter old lady, and I don't want to be that person. I've just got to get some good sleep."

As June calms down, more information comes out about what is bothering her.

Fay: "Oh my! You're losing sleep! So much so that you don't even recognize yourself. June, this must be awful. You've been holding things in to be kind to me."

Fay is tempted to apologize but doesn't want to interrupt June by trying to make things better, so she continues reflecting.

June: [almost in tears] "Yes, I'm sorry. I hate to complain. I hate complainers. And now I am one. I keep thinking it will get better but it hasn't. I really can't take it anymore. I just don't know what to do about it."

> *June is now concerned with Fay's perspective. Her being able to take another's perspective means that she is being less self-absorbed and more of her normal, responsive self.*

Fay: "Yes, let's discuss what to do about it. But I first want to tell you how sorry I am. I had no idea about this. I am so sorry, June, for all of your lost sleep. This has been a real nightmare for you! Thank you for being honest with me. I can see it was hard for you to come to me. Is there more for me to know?"

> *Fay apologizes before they move forward to discuss ways to remedy the situation. She also asks June again if there is more she'd like to talk about. This is a great example of wringing out the washcloth, as discussed in chapter 2.*

June: "Yes, I was worried. I don't want to lose your friendship. It means the world to me."

The conversation now has a regular tone. This situation might continue on in a variety of ways. June and Fay might sit down for tea together to discuss how to move forward. They might struggle to find a workable solution, or June or Fay might get triggered and upset again—then one of them can begin the Gesture. Or they might come up with an innovative solution, such as June taking care of the dog on nights when Fay has to work. Perhaps June can't have a dog of her own because it would be too much for her to care for, but she would love to have a visitor a few nights a week. Creative solutions happen when people are feeling connected.

> **Creative solutions happen when people are feeling connected.**

Notice that Fay is not trying to control June's reactions nor change her perceptions. She is only trying to give June the feeling of getting listened to and to do this until June is completely finished. In the end, Fay doesn't feel defensive, even though at the beginning she may have had the temptation to defend herself by saying, "I don't have any choice about my hours," or "How could I have known this? You waited so long to tell me." Fay may have the opportunity to tell June about the things she had already done to keep the dog from barking or about her own dissatisfaction with her work schedule, but based on the Gesture, this can surface, if she chooses, during their regular discussion, not while June is upset.

Overall, notice the unpredictable nature of the exchange. Emotions go up and down, and when the Gesture is happening, there is no telling which way the speaker will head. The more the speaker feels assured that they will indeed feel heard, the more they are likely to calm down, be conversational, and be responsive in return.

Climbing the Ladder

The Gesture is a dynamic process, where small and large changes can happen in any moment. People calm down, people get riled up, people feel emotional—it requires the listener to adapt and be resilient while giving someone the feeling of getting listened to. The process of achieving the Gesture is like climbing a ladder toward empathic listening. Think of the Gesture as a ladder that you climb over and over again.

> Sometimes it's a little better to travel than to arrive.
>
> —Robert M. Pirsig,
> *Zen and the Art of Motorcycle Maintenance*

> One can choose to go back toward safety or forward toward growth. Growth must be chosen again and again; fear must be overcome again and again.
>
> —Abraham Maslow,
> American psychologist

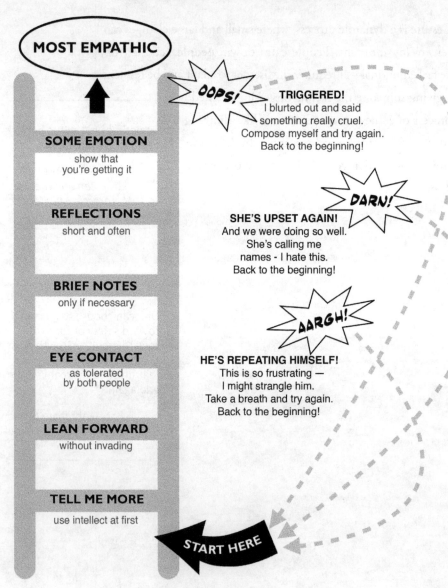

Here is my own thought process regarding how I think about the ladder: As a conversation heats up, I decide to begin using the Gesture. This is the moment where I designate myself to be the listener, which allows the other person to be the speaker. This is the bottom rung of the ladder where I find the impulse to say, "Tell me more," in the face of the speaker being despondent or aggressive. I remain engaged and I lean forward. I begin by using *safety net statements* and *quick phrase reflections*. I might say, "Wow, you've had it!" or "This has been horrible." The speaker might sound bitter or mean but I know to expect this, because when people are upset they act upset. And I think, *Ooh! I am supposed to lean forward*, so I change my stance to be even softer, more concerned, more empathic. Now I am feeling it. I feel empathy for the speaker. I feel proud of getting to this point.

As the speaker begins to talk with fewer expletives and in more complete and coherent sentences, I start making *short list reflections* to make sure that the speaker feels listened to. I intend to do this until the speaker is all-the-way done.

> There's no need to be perfect to inspire others. Let people get inspired by how you deal with your imperfections.
>
> – Ziad K. Abdelnour,
> *Economic Warfare*

Suddenly something happens: The speaker says just one more thing, and I blurt out, "Who are *you* to talk?" or "This is so ridiculous! You have such a double standard." Responding to my outburst, the speaker revs up and says something like, "See, you're a jerk! You're proving my point!" or closes down and says, "Never mind, I'm outta here!" I think, *Darn, that isn't how I want to be.* So I go back to the beginning, to the bottom rung, and say, "Sorry, I blew it. I really want to listen and I'm trying to do better. Please do tell me more."

I continue this process until the speaker is completely finished. I tell myself this: I am human and I will blow it some of the time *and* I will also succeed much of the time. It is OK to make a mistake as long as I don't let it derail me. I give myself the same permission to be fallible as I do the speaker. I find empathy for myself, and then I climb the ladder again. So I say, "Tell me more," and sure enough, the speaker does just that.

■　■　■

Being imperfect and then forgiving yourself are important. We are not robots, nor do we desire to achieve that sort of rigid perfection. We are human, and being human while trying to give a person the feeling of getting listened to is part of the Gesture. Although failure is a necessary part of learning and growing, it often comes with its own triggers. It means embarrassment, shame, feeling less than—we might even have experienced someone withdrawing their love when we failed them. This is some pretty heavy stuff. So remember this: Count on failing. Failing is part of practice, and the Gesture is a practice. It is humanly difficult, yet certainly attainable, to exhibit empathy when someone is raging and pushing our trigger buttons. You must expect to fail along the way, and in doing so, not only do you learn, but also you demonstrate and embrace your vulnerability. This is part of making and maintaining human connection.

> From failing you learn – from success, not so much!
>
> – Aunt Billie,
> *Meet the Robinsons*

After failing or making a mistake, you then have the opportunity to demonstrate your resilience by forgiving yourself and getting back to climbing the ladder. The symbolism of climbing is important. The

Gesture is not a stagnant place that we attain. We don't perch at the top, arms folded, thinking we have arrived. The conversation is continually changing, so we are constantly being tested. We are striving, or climbing, to be our best, empathic selves.

The Larger Conversation

Let's face it: Leaning forward and saying, "Tell me more" in normal dialogue could get annoying to both participants. Imagine two people leaning forward to each other constantly saying, "Tell me more," reflecting what the other has said, and being incessantly attentive. How horrible! The Gesture is not a style of communication that is used in everyday conversation. Although there are many lessons to be learned that will benefit your everyday conversation, the intensive reflecting is not for ordinary use.

> The world is not imperfect or slowly evolving along a path to perfection. No, it is perfect at every moment, every sin already carries grace in it.
>
> – Hermann Hesse, German-born Swiss novelist

In everyday conversation, we might listen quietly for extended periods. We might interrupt each other with new ideas or excitement or concerns. We accept and enjoy these natural ebbs and flows in our conversation because we are accustomed to the patterns—they are comforting and connecting.

When conflict arises, as it will, we decide to welcome it. We disagree or feel hurt, and therefore, quite suddenly, we move from normal conversation into conflict conversation, the *Tell Me More Gesture*. We stop talking, sit forward, say, "Tell me more," and make reflections.

We do this until the other person is all-the-way done. We do not know if this will take a few minutes or an hour—or more.

After being listened to, the speaker might feel curious or open to hearing your point of view, but we can't control this, nor can we count on it. You take a break, to create some contemplative silence, to let the speaker's message sink in more deeply, to determine if you are wanting to be the speaker in this conflict conversation, and to collect your thoughts.

> The turning point in the process of growing up is when you discover the core of strength within you that survives all hurt.
>
> – Max Lerner,
> Russian-born American journalist

If the conflict is over, then you go back to the larger conversation. You are no longer practicing the Gesture. Now you might sit back in your chair and converse routinely. If conflict arises again, you sit forward and engage more. This is the Gesture in the context of the larger conversation.

Difficult People (and Other Doubts)

In the backs of everyone's minds, whether while reading this book or participating in a workshop, scenes are being played out from the past. We are thinking about specific times where the situation (or the other person) is too horrible, too crazy, too far gone to use the Gesture. Following are some of the common doubts that people feel regarding the impossibility or inappropriateness of the Gesture to their personal situations.

High-conflict people

Unfortunately for the mediation profession, it has become popular to blame people who do not collaborate or compromise on their being high-conflict people or difficult people.

> High-conflict people (HCPs) have a pattern of high-conflict behavior that increases conflict rather than reducing it or resolving it. This pattern usually happens over and over again in many different situations with many different people. The issue that seems in conflict at the time is not what is increasing the conflict. The "issue" is not the issue. With HCPs the high-conflict pattern of behavior is the issue, including a lot of: (A) All-or-nothing thinking, (B) Unmanaged emotions, (C) Extreme behaviors, (D) Blaming others (Eddy 2012, 1).

The author further explains that the issue is not what is inflaming the conflict. This is, of course, true more often than not. This notion is not exclusive to so-called HCPs. People are commonly not upset with only the issue at hand. They usually have a variety of past issues and carry this baggage into the conversation without ever mentioning it. People are also upset about the way they were treated. The issue is rarely the issue, or at least rarely the *only* issue.

Judging and blaming people for acting upset, as the notion of HCPs does, only increases the conflict. We

> When people appear to be something other than good and decent, it is only because they are reacting to stress, pain, or the deprivation of basic human needs such as security, love, and self-esteem.
>
> – Abraham Maslow, American psychologist

understand that all-or-nothing thinking, unmanaged emotions, extreme behaviors, and blaming others are all understandable attributes of how people behave in conflict. We do not criticize or blame them in return. We give them the opportunity to say more instead of shutting them down, and we let them know that we will listen to them until they are all-the-way done.

> Even if [people] have learned the basics of a win-win approach to negotiation, when placed in situations of conflict, they revert back to costly and destructive win-lose methods, usually attributing this reversion to the necessity of dealing with difficult people.
>
> —William Ury,
> *Getting to Yes With Yourself*

In general, labeling people is an obstruction to the communication and to the connection we are trying to create. Once we label someone, whether the label be HCP, difficult, crazy, immovable, narcissistic, sociopathic, etc, we inevitably stop listening with an open mind; we stop taking them seriously; and we start making assumptions based on their label. Our categorization of their behaviors becomes a self-fulfilling cycle of judgment and blame.

The only good reason for using a label in conflict is to use it to find empathy for the person, to find deeper understanding of their experience so that we can open up to them, not close them down. If it helps to know that a person, for example, has a habit of lashing out, we can then find more patience for them and open ourselves up to new ways of listening.

I hear you telling me now that I am being Pollyanna about this, that there are indeed people who are just plain difficult, who crave conflict and pouring abuse on others. OK, let's assume this is true. Think now specifically about a person you feel is an HCP. Think about the topics that are upsetting for them. Think about how you are treated.

So consider this: Your best chance for a good outcome, HCP or no HCP, is to employ the Gesture in the most connecting, empathic manner you can muster.

People who repeat themselves

Although we attribute the characteristic to self-centeredness, being stuck, or not being able to leave a subject, people who repeat themselves generally do so for a good reason: They don't feel heard. As a mediator, if someone has repeated themselves three times or more, I will sometimes place my hands on the table in front of me to stop them for a moment, and I transparently say something like this: "Gary, I've heard you say that you've had it with being in charge. You feel responsible for everyone and you need help. You've come back to this several times in the session—I bet you've said it four times. I have to believe that if you felt like we were hearing you, you wouldn't keep saying it. So I'm wondering if you could say more about this—what are we missing?" Notice I am by no means telling Gary to stop repeating himself. I am actually inviting him to say more about the topic.

> To listen is very hard, because it asks of us so much interior stability that we no longer need to prove ourselves by speeches, arguments, statements or declarations. True listeners no longer have an inner need to make their presence known. They are free to receive, welcome, to accept.
>
> – Henry Nouwen,
> Dutch Catholic priest

You can do the same thing in the Gesture. Try saying something like this: "Judy, I've heard you say <u>that I dropped the ball on the project</u> three or four times. I have to assume you wouldn't repeat this if you felt like I was really hearing you. What am I missing?" You may insert your pertinent information in the underlined sections.

Being a doormat

In nearly every workshop I have led, a participant says that they would feel like a doormat if they take on the Gesture, and they usually have a particular person (who tromps on them) in mind. My question is, *What are the alternatives?* You can refuse to have the conversation at all because you don't like the way you are getting treated, or you can interrupt them to tell them to stop their annoying, mean behaviors. When the participant tells me this is what they have tried in the past, I ask if it has helped. They always say that it has not helped. Their conversations with this person continue to be unsatisfying because they are always getting talked over and demeaned.

> Sometimes it's not the strength but the gentleness that cracks the hardest shells.
>
> – Richard Paul Evans, *Lost December*

Know this: The Gesture is not meant to encourage you to just take whatever someone dishes out. In fact, the Gesture teaches you to be actively engaged in what they are dishing out. This is what will keep you from feeling and looking like a doormat. You may find that there is, eventually, a very different reaction from the person who is constantly interrupting, talking over, belittling, etc. This also will provide the opportunity for the "doormat person" to feel strong and satisfied and for both parties to feel connected.

Other inhibitors to communication

There are indeed many factors that make communication more difficult. Here are a few: narcissism, alcoholism or addiction of any kind, borderline personality disorder, racism, sexism, elitism, bullying, shaming, threatening—the list is endless. First of all, let's admit that when we are upset we are more likely to diagnose and label the other person. That is, they look less normal when we're triggered. But let's assume, for the moment, that the category in which we have placed the person is accurate, and note the following four truths about the labels:

1. We all are likely on the spectrum of at least one, if not many, of these inhibitors/diagnoses/attributes. Therefore, here is an opportunity for empathy. I too am imperfect.

2. What has worked well for you in the past when communicating during conflict with these people? Stopping them? Talking over them? Blaming them? If whatever you have been doing has not produced satisfying results, why not try something that might begin a change? Don't write them off. Use the attribute as a cue to go deeper into listening. Make sure that they are feeling listened to by asking them to tell you more.

3. If you interrupt them to get heard or shut them down, you are now doing the exact thing that you detest about their behavior. You must realize that you very well may not get heard. That is information for you.

> I don't like to arrange things. If I stand in front of something, instead of arranging it, I arrange myself.
>
> —Diane Arbus, American photographer

4. It is not your job to hang in there with people who treat you badly, but if you are going to try to communicate, especially during conflict, the Gesture is your best bet.

You can benefit from using the Gesture during conflict with absolutely anyone with whom you choose to have a relationship. You may consider a relationship anything that fits *your* definition—romantic partner, work colleague, neighbor, retail worker, or even perfect stranger. These are people who are acting angry, interrupting, won't calm down, won't get to the point, are completely unreasonable, and/or won't compromise. The Gesture means that we are telling people, explicitly through our actions and words, that we understand why they might be angry, interrupting, and unable to calm down, and we welcome their imperfections.

Moving Forward

In chapter 9, we have looked at the Gesture as a whole, using a ladder as an analogy for the overall manner and mindset to adopt during conflict. The notion of climbing the ladder is a reminder that the Gesture is a process that is rarely static or predictable, but is, actually, constantly changing as emotions go up and down. We expect this and learn that we are resilient and that feeling connected during conflict is a new reward.

Journal Entry 9.1

Consider the ladder on page 210. Notice in particular the exclamations on the right side where people fall off the ladder. Think about two or three people who you know can have this effect on you. Perhaps they are at home or at work, or perhaps a friend or a relative. First, write, very specifically, about the things these people say or do that would tumble you off the ladder.

_____

_____

_____

_____

_____

_____

_____

Next, come up with some ideas of ways that you can handle these situations that would be in line with the values of the Gesture. How can you find and show empathy for them?

_____

_____

_____

_____

_____

_____

_____

_____

Journal Entry 9.2

First, list three or four of your favorite aspects of the Gesture. What is most exciting to you?

_____

_____

_____

_____

_____

Next, write about your doubts. What is keeping you from wholeheartedly embracing the Gesture?

_____

_____

_____

_____

Lastly, look back at your favorite aspects. Is there advice that your excited self can give to your doubting self?

_____

_____

_____

_____

_____

Chapter 10:
MAKING CHANGE

The *Tell Me More Gesture* requires and promotes change in many ways. While change involves the unknown, and therefore can be an intimidating idea, it is also exciting and inspiring.

> It's time again. Tear up the violets and plant something more difficult to grow.
>
> —James Schuyler,
> American poet

Welcoming Change

The *Tell Me More Gesture* is a gesture of truly welcoming conflict, which is essentially the same as welcoming change and the unknown. Welcoming conflict and change means understanding that there is something worthwhile on the other side of the temporary chaos that often is present during a transformative process. We welcome conflict and change because we believe that a process that embraces openness, nonjudgment, and empathy will ultimately result in the best outcome. We cannot predetermine the best result because the process itself determines it.

> Faith is the bird that feels the light and sings when the dawn is still dark.
>
> —Rabindranath Tagore,
> Bengalese poet

Trusting the process is a big leap for many people. We come to a discussion with needed and desired results, and the Gesture involves letting go of those, at least temporarily, so that we can remain open to unknown results. Letting go of outcomes requires a faith in the process and, until you have experienced it, faith can be hard to find. This is a bit of a dilemma: How do you find the faith to let go of outcomes, reserve judgments, and be open to new discoveries? The answer is that you do it in baby steps, and the first baby step is to lean forward and say, "Tell me more."

Changing Your Self

The concept of leaning toward a person who is yelling at you and saying to them, "Tell me more," is uncomfortable at first, maybe even scary. Making reflections so that people can feel listened to until they are all-the-way done, even when they are spewing hateful comments, is a new way of communicating during conflict. Obviously, the Gesture requires you to make significant change to your self.

> Even though you may have an internal resistance to change, you also have a natural inclination toward growth.
>
> —Schlitz, Vieten & Amorok, *Living Deeply*

Making change is neither easy nor automatic. Taking on the Gesture entails making a conscious shift in your belief system about communication, perhaps also to your worldview. Your own needs remain important, but you are taking the larger, longer view. Your needs are not merely to have your own views heard. They include being involved in a process that gives you self-respect, deepens your own understanding of a situation, and keeps you feeling connected.

Notice that only one thing has changed for you to make the Gesture a success: your response to conflict. In the *Power of Habit* (2014), Duhigg uses the term *routine*. He notes that in order to change a routine (or a habit), the cue (or trigger) remains the same, and the reward (or payoff) remains the same. So to change an unwanted habit, you need to replace it with something that will produce the same reward.

In the case of the Gesture, the conflict is the cue, the undesirable conflict response (lashing out, defending, problem-solving, shutting down, or pretending to listen) is the routine, and the reward, although different for each of us, is, at a minimum, to make the problem go away. The "problem" could be a variety of things, such as a disagreement, how someone is getting treated, hurt feelings, etc. The chart below depicts this relationship.

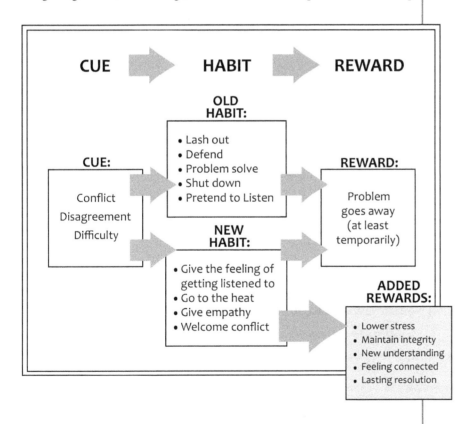

Here the old conflict responses, the old routine, are replaced with the Gesture. Notice that there are many additional rewards when you change the routine to the Gesture. The key to establishing the new routine is to practice until it becomes completely automatic. Duhigg (2014) also notes that to accomplish the change in routine, we must believe that it is possible. Utilizing this book completely, with its skills, exercises, journal entries, stories, and inspirational quotes, helps you believe it is possible, and thus begins the process of the Gesture becoming an automatic routine.

> People only seriously consider change when they feel accepted for exactly who they are.
>
> —Carl Rogers,
> American psychologist

But beware: As humans, we tend to tailor new information and experiences to fit into our current way of thinking. Rather than broadening our perspective, we naturally squeeze the new information into our worldview. There is a temptation to take in only parts of new information, or to do so in an insubstantial way, so that we do not have to feel challenged. When we don't enlarge our framework to deeply accommodate new experiences, we then tend to hold even stronger to our original, cherished worldview (Schlitz, Vieten, and Amorok 2007).

There is a natural human inclination to reject new information, so we shove the nonconforming aspects aside and think, *My situation is different—this doesn't apply to me*, or *Well, yeah, I agree—to a point*, or *I already do something fairly close to that*. There are a million ways to defend not making change. Each of us struggles with the same temptation to stay safe and not be challenged; the opportunity missed is for ourselves.

But here's a great irony of our humanness: We are change averse *and* we are drawn toward growth. Learning new things and having new experiences makes us feel engaged and vibrant. When we are deliberate and courageous about change we can take in new ways of thinking, doing, and being that are life altering.

Changing Others

Let's just admit it: When we are in conflict, what we really want is for the other person to change. We think to ourselves, *I'm going to learn the Gesture, but they are the ones who really need it. I'm already a pretty good listener.* Even when we are not in conflict, it is often our deepest wish that the other person would be a better communicator. *If only they would listen to me. If only they would change in the same ways I have.* Alas, we know that we only control ourselves. While understanding this is empowering, our wishes for the other to change are often unfulfilled, which is disappointing. Here's the amazing thing: The more you work on yourself, the more resolute you are to adopt the Gesture and to not blame the other for your behaviors or inability to be an incredible listener, the greater the chance that the other person will also make some changes. We can't make it happen, it can't be our goal, but it is a byproduct that often occurs. "When? When will it happen?" I hear you ask.

> If we wait for the other person to change, we may spend all our time waiting. So it's better that you change yourself. Don't try to force the other person to change. Even if it takes a long time, you will feel better when you are master of yourself and you are doing your best.
>
> —Thích Nhất Hanh,
> *The Art of Communicating*

■ ■ ■

When my children were very young they were sweet playmates. Rachel is three years older than Adam, and they used to spend hours under the dining room table or in the bottom bunk of their bed hanging cloths and blankets and playing imaginary characters and scenes. When Rachel had friends over to play they automatically included Adam in whatever they were doing. When Rachel turned thirteen, things changed. She wanted to be with her friends separately and had little time for her brother. Suddenly everything he did drove her crazy. She was often unkind and dismissive. When Rachel was seventeen, she began wanting to change their interactions. She didn't like how Adam treated her. Rachel was not consistent in her desire, but she knew she didn't like the way it was going. She began treating him more kindly and including him more often with her friends. At this point, Adam, now fourteen, had developed completely different habits with her. He was used to mistreating her, and now he was of an age where he was relishing his independence from her. She ran to me one day after she had said something to him that was kind and patient, and he had responded snidely. She was upset he didn't respond nicely to her. I told her their way of being together had worsened over several years, and she might have to be more consistently kind and inclusive for his behavior to change, too. She left in a huff, wanting him to make the change right away.

■ ■ ■

Ultimately, Adam did respond to Rachel's newfound patience and kindness, but this happened gradually over several years. It is completely normal for children to go through this, and it is completely understandable in adults as well. Making change toward better communication involves trust and self-awareness. We can help build trust by being consistent in our own behaviors, but we cannot force a person to become self-aware nor to recognize the changes we have made in ourselves. This must happen in their own way and in their own time. Honestly, it may never happen.

People need to find their own desire and their own motivation for change. We can share the book, but we can't make them read it.

■   ■   ■

A couple, Randy and Eleanor, came in for a private conflict workshop. At Eleanor's request, they had each been reading a self-help book about emotionally focused therapy (EFT). Eleanor was distraught because, although Randy had committed, he had not kept up on reading the book. They decided during our session that they would, twice a week, read the book to each other and discuss the topics and exercises. On a return visit, Eleanor was visibly upset. One of her sources of distress was the book issue. She exclaimed during their session, "We're reading it aloud, discussing the exercises at length, and I don't see any improvement!"

■   ■   ■

In this case, Eleanor indeed could make Randy read the book, but she couldn't make him change. I spent several sessions with Eleanor and Randy, helping them each to learn more about and practice the Gesture. They both ultimately did make changes, but it was on separate time frames and with different motivations.

Conflict Transformation

The Gesture requires changing one's thinking from dealing with conflict, what some call conflict resolution, to welcoming conflict, which can be called conflict transformation. We are changing conversations by focusing on the process, not the outcome, by transforming the conflict from an alienating experience to a connecting experience.

This book offers a solid introduction to the *Tell Me More Gesture*. There is a lot to assimilate. Some of the ideas and information might make intuitive sense. Some of it might be shocking or sound impossible. While it is difficult, it is far from impossible. The best way to learn it is to *do* it. We learn to swim by swimming, and we learn to give the feeling of getting listened to by doing it.

> We learn to swim by swimming, and we learn to give someone the feeling of getting listened to by doing it.

Remember that finding the impulse comes first, and then finding the courage to say, "Tell me more," is the beginning of a positive conflict communication cycle, the conflict transformation. This is a practice. We never perfect it because we are beautifully human. It is our humanity that enables us to find and express empathy for someone in a very difficult, and sometimes ugly, state. We begin working on the

Gesture to find ways to communicate during conflict with our loved ones, and we then begin to use it with people at work, in our neighborhoods, or even with perfect strangers.

Social Change

The *Tell Me More Gesture* has great potential for positive impact on one's community and our larger society. The Gesture provides the possibility for attitudinal change about conflict. When people have new and ongoing success welcoming difficult discussions, they learn to not fear, nor avoid, nor react to difficult discussions and topics, which opens their world to new possibilities about what to do and how to behave when a person is upset. The mere change of not fearing difficult interactions means that people feel calmer. They can greet the world feeling more empowered and more likely to be responsive to others' needs, opinions, and wishes. There is a huge potential for a ripple effect as people learn to greet conflict with openness and empathy.

As discussed in chapter 2, the Gesture is a practice that relies on a relational worldview, that is, that people are in the world balancing their need for independence with their need for being connected to others. The practice of utilizing the Gesture not only is based on this worldview, but it also encourages and cultivates a change in worldview to a relational belief system, based on the connection it promotes. For example, people who believe in an individualistic worldview might learn the Gesture merely in order

> We think we listen, but very rarely do we listen with real understanding, true empathy. Yet listening, of this very special kind, is one of the most potent forces for change that I know.
>
> —Carl Rogers,
> American psychologist

> When you make a world tolerable for yourself, you make a world tolerable for others.
>
> – Anaïs Nin,
> French memoirist & feminist

to feel calmer and clearer during conflict. Their personal success using the model helps them feel new bonds and closeness that they might otherwise not experience. This begins a new cycle of connectedness during conflict, which expands exponentially each time it is used, and thus, passed on.

If we expand this idea to include people who strongly disagree with each other about hot, polarizing topics, there is an immense opportunity for a new way of communicating.

■   ■   ■

Toward the end of a workshop in 2015, a woman posed a thoughtful question to me that I had never considered. She asked, "What about hate speech? What if you hear someone disrespecting Muslims, for example? Isn't it our duty to speak out against this?" My answer to her was this: What would happen if you leaned forward and said to them, "Tell me more?" What would that feel like to them? What might you learn about that person? What might they learn about themselves, as they are welcomed to say more about something that is abhorrent to the other? How could you find empathy for them? There is one thing I am sure of: In a one-on-one conversation, shutting people down will not change their point of view. Judging them for what they believe is likely to corner them into holding onto their notions even more firmly.

We peace people have always listened to the oppressed and disenfranchised. One of the steps we should take is to listen to those we consider "the enemy" with the same openness, non-judgment, and compassion, we listen to those with whom our sympathies lie.

– Gene Knudsen Hoffman,
Compassionate Listening

■   ■   ■

People talk about peace in one breath and shut people down in the next. We cannot make peace by talking over people. We must find a way to maintain or create a feeling of connectedness. We can only do this by listening deeply with the intention of truly finding a new understanding. We must give others the feeling of getting listened to until they are all-the-way done.

What if instead of recommending that people talk to each other, we start recommending that people listen with each other? We could communicate about social issues, economic issues, political issues, and more because we expect to listen, we expect to give recognition, and we expect to learn new things. When we truly listen with empathy, making sure that the speaker feels listened to, the discussion doesn't get easier, it gets more productive.

> **When we listen with empathy, making sure that the speaker feels listened to, the discussion doesn't get easier, it gets more productive.**

■ ■ ■

Henry, a friend of our family, grew up in a very strict, right wing, ultra-conservative Christian home and now considers himself to be socially and politically progressive. According to him, his parents were part of the most extreme sect he knew. He would go door to door spreading the religious gospel based on these strict, and rather bizarre, tenets. Henry said that some people would walk away or shut the door in his face; this did *not* help him to change and get out from the weight of the burdensome dogma he was espousing. He told us that the thing that changed him was that some people were kind to him and would patiently listen to him. They would strike up a conversation, and it always started with his feeling listened to. The act of *not* rejecting him based on his beliefs, and actually including and valuing him as a person, was the act that opened him up to new ways of thinking.

■ ■ ■

This inspiring story demonstrates that Henry's ability to make change in his own life was facilitated by people who truly listened to him and welcomed his point of view, even though they were opposite in their beliefs. Although they disagreed, Henry could feel that they cared for him as a person, even though they were strangers. This is a wonderful example of using the Gesture and welcoming an unpopular way of thinking in order to have a connecting, and potentially life-changing, experience.

Moving Forward

We are all suffering when we are in conflict. We all dream of getting listened to until we are all-the-way done—in a way that we can really feel listened to. Nothing would feel better than this. Remarkably, the next best thing to receiving it is giving it. You will find that the more you give it, the less you will need to receive it. This is not immediate; it takes a lot of practice, and then we become changed and we move forward.

> It's no use going back to yesterday. I was a different person then.
>
> – Lewis Carroll,
> *Alice in Wonderland*

We begin to experience something deeper, more connecting, where we do not need to harm in return, we do not need to protect ourselves, and we do not need to have our say during the height of a conflict. Personally, this has had a larger effect on myself, on my own behavior, and on my belief system than anyone could have given me by giving me the gift of getting listened to. Of course, I still like to get listened to, but I crave giving the Gesture more than receiving it. This was an unintentional gift to myself.

As you practice the *Tell Me More Gesture* by opening up the conversation, reserving judgment, finding empathy, and starting it over and over again, you will find yourself traveling on a new road unlike anything you have experienced in the past. This is not an easier road. This is a deeper, more connecting path that enables relationships to be maintained, repaired, and enriched during hard times.

Using the Gesture and welcoming conflict is connecting and healing. I see it with people in my office, in my workshops, in my family, and I see it in myself. Balance in conflict communication means you set your sights on listening, not 50 percent of the time, but nearly all of the time. Balance in conflict communication means you move almost exclusively to giving recognition, to the Gesture. It changes the course of the discussion for you, the listener, and for the speaker, and it maintains and encourages connection during an incredibly difficult time, and thus begins real change in the world.

> And so try listening. Listen to your wife, your husband, your father, your mother, your children, your friends, to those who love you and those who don't, to those who bore you, to your enemies. It will work a small miracle. And perhaps a great one.
>
> —Brenda Ueland,
> *Strength To Your Sword Arm*

REFERENCES AND RESOURCES

Brown, Brené. 2010. *The Gifts of Imperfection: Let Go of Who You Think You're Supposed to Be and Embrace Who You Are*. Center City, MN: Hazelden.

Bush, Robert A. Baruch, and Joseph P. Folger. 2005. *The Promise of Mediation: The Transformative Approach to Conflict*. San Francisco: Jossey-Bass.

Bushman, Brad J. 2002. "Does Venting Anger Feed or Extinguish the Flame? Catharsis, Rumination, Distraction, Anger, and Aggressive Responding." *Personality and Social Psychology Bulletin* 28 (6): 724-31. doi:10.1177/0146167202289002.

Columbia Counseling Center, Comprehensive Psychological & Psychiatric Services. 2010. "Couples Communication: The Rules." Accessed November 10, 2016. https://www. counselingmaryland.com/2010/07/23/couples-communication-strategies/.

CRC Health Group. n.d. "Drug Therapy What Is It?" Accessed November 10, 2016. http:// www.crchealth.com/types-of-therapy/what-is-drug-therapy/.

Duhigg, Charles. 2014. *The Power of Habit: Why We Do What We Do in Life and in Business*. New York: Random House Trade Paperbacks.

EBBP.org. n.d. "Exposure Therapy and CBT for Anxiety Disorders: Frequently Asked Questions." Accessed November 10, 2016. http://www.ebbp.org/resources/Anxiety_ExposureTherapyandCBT_FAQ.pdf.

Eddy, Bill. 2012. "Who Are High Conflict People?" High Conflict Institute. Accessed November 10, 2016. http://www.highconflictinstitute.com/who-are-high-conflict-people.

EMDRIA. n.d. "What is the actual EMDR session like?" EMDR International Association. Accessed November 10, 2016. http://www.emdria.org/general/custom.asp?page=120.

Goldsmith, Marshall, and Mark Reiter. 2015. *Triggers: Creating Behavior That Lasts—Becoming the Person You Want to Be.* New York: Crown Publishing Group.

Goldstein, David. 2009. "Walter Cannon: Homeostasis, the Fight-or-Flight Response, the Sympathoadrenal System, and the Wisdom of the Body." BrainImmune: Trends in Neuroendocrine Immunology. Accessed November 10, 2016. http://www.brainimmune.com/walter-cannon-homeostasis-the-fight-or-flight-response-the-sympathoadrenal-system-and-the-wisdom-of-the-body/.

GoodTherapy.org. n.d. "Activities, Types, and Tips to Find." Accessed November 10, 2016. https://www.goodtherapy.org/learn-about-therapy/modes/group-therapy.

Hạnh, Nhất. 2011. *True Love: A Practice for Awakening the Heart.* Boston: Shambhala.

Hạnh, Nhất. 2013. *The Art of Communicating.* New York: HarperCollins Publishers.

Myers, Isabel Briggs. 1980. *Gifts Differing.* Palo Alto, CA: Consulting Psychologists Press.

National Association of Cognitive-Behavioral Therapists. n.d. "Why Cognitive-Behavioral Therapy (CBT)?" Accessed November 10, 2016. http://www.nacbt.org/whycbt-htm/.

National Hypnotherapy Society. n.d. "What Is Hypnotherapy?" Accessed November 10, 2016. http://www.nationalhypnotherapysociety.org/therapists/about/.

Noba. n.d. "Judgment and Decision Making." Accessed November 10, 2016. http://nobaproject.com/modules/judgment-and-decision-making.

Psych Central. 2016. "About Behavior Therapy." Accessed November 10, 2016. https://psychcentral.com/lib/about-behavior-therapy/.

Rodgers, Carl R. 1980. *A Way of Being*. Boston: Houghton Mifflin Company.

Rosenberg, Marshall B. 2015. *Nonviolent Communication: A Language of Life*. Encinitas, CA: Puddledancer Press.

Rowe, Crayton E., and David S. MacIsaac. 1989. *Empathic Attunement: The "Technique" of Psychoanalytic Self Psychology*. Northvale, NJ: Jason Aronson.

Sasscer-Burgos, Julie. 2014. "Our Brains on Conflict: A Neuroscience Explanation." Accessed December 10, 2017. https://www.adr.gov/events/2014/our-brains-on-conflict-feb2014.pdf.

Schlitz, Marilyn, Cassandra Vieten, and Tina Amorok. 2007. *Living Deeply: The Art & Science of Transformation in Everyday Life*. Oakland, CA: New Harbinger Publications.

Seligman, Martin E. 2011. *Flourish*. New York: Free Press.

Shedler, Jonathan. 2010. "The Efficacy of Psychodynamic Psychotherapy." *American Psychologist* 63 (2): 98-109. https://www.apa.org/pubs/journals/releases/amp-65-2-98.pdf.

Ueland, Brenda. 1993. *Strength to Your Sword Arm: Selected Writings*. Duluth, MN: Holy Cow! Press.

Vermilyea, Elizabeth. G. 2013. *Growing Beyond Survival: A Self-Help Toolkit for Managing Traumatic Stress*. Baltimore, MD: The Sidran Institute Press.

Watterson, Kathryn. 1995. *Not by the Sword: How the Love of a Cantor and His Family Transformed a Klansman*. New York: Simon & Schuster.

Yoder, Carolyn. 2005. *The Little Book of Trauma Healing: When Violence Strikes and Community Security Is Threatened*. Intercourse, PA: Good Books.

Zander, Rosamund Stone, and Benjamin Zander. 2002. *The Art of Possibility: Transforming Professional and Personal Life*. Boston: Harvard Business School Press.

ABOUT THE AUTHOR

In her mediation practice, Janet Rowles specializes in high conflict and emotionally difficult situations. Janet teaches the *Tell Me More Gesture* in workshops and speaking engagements. She trains mediators and other professionals in her workshops, *Dealing with High Conflict* and *Inclusivity in Group Facilitation.* A Minnesota native, her professional studies include a B.A. from Colorado College, a certificate in Dispute Resolution from Mitchell-Hamline Dispute Resolution Institute, and a M.A. in Human Development from St. Mary's University of Minnesota. Janet is trained in transformative mediation, eldercare mediation, circle keeping, and the social inclusion method for bullying in schools. Janet does small and large group work including circle-keeping and facilitating group discussions such as condo associations and non-profit board decision-making. Janet has been a volunteer-mediator for Conflict Resolution Center in Minneapolis since 2003 and was a board member there from 2004-2011. In 2013, Janet received a Peacemaker of the Year award from Minneapolis Public Schools for her circle work with pregnant and parenting teens. Janet was the videographer and voice behind the viral cellphone video of a police incident with an African-American pedestrian in 2016.

CPSIA information can be obtained
at www.ICGtesting.com
Printed in the USA
FSHW02n2152060718
50076FS